Whitehead's Metaphysics

A Critical Examination

of *Process and Reality*

Whitehead's Metaphysics

A Critical Examination
of *Process and Reality*
by Edward Pols

Southern Illinois University Press   *Carbondale and Edwardsville*

Feffer & Simons, Inc.   *London and Amsterdam*

PREFACE

THE PURPOSE of this book is a modest one. It is, first of all, concerned primarily with those aspects of Whitehead's philosophy that belong to traditional metaphysics, and thus deals only glancingly with those parts of *Process and Reality* in which Whitehead attempts to apply his metaphysics to an interpretation of physical reality as revealed in twentieth century physics. This is an important omission in dealing with a book whose subtitle is *An Essay in Cosmology* and whose themes so often echo those of Plato's *Timaeus*. Second, the present book is limited to an examination of *Process and Reality,* except where certain doctrines of *Science and the Modern World* and, to a lesser degree, *Adventures of Ideas* and *Modes of Thought* seem to illuminate difficulties in Whitehead's chief metaphysical work. Finally, although I trust I have had something to say about most of Whitehead's doctrines that are clearly metaphysical, I have made the problem of freedom my chief concern, hoping in this way to cast an intense if narrow beam on the structure of his metaphysical system. The organization of *Process and Reality*—a summary statement of a number of doctrines that are meant to be (in Whitehead's special sense) coherent, followed by a more detailed exposition and application of these doctrines—makes the choice of one important theme to traverse and retraverse Whitehead's metaphysics a good one for both expository and critical purposes.

I have not found it either possible or desirable to separate exposition from criticism and commentary. Thus, although the first two chapters are largely expository, the major critical themes, which must in any case partly dictate the expository emphasis, are already adumbrated there. And the sustained criticism, to which the later chapters are devoted, is accomplished largely by way of a much more searching and detailed expository analysis of material introduced in the first two chapters. Since the criticism is as much an internal criticism as I was capable of making it, the technique of detailed expository analysis must be the chief critical instrument anyway. I have, in effect, only been inquiring whether the parts of Whitehead's system support each other in the way in which they were intended to—whether, that is, Whitehead has succeeded in devising or imagining a system that sustains the concreteness of what, in some moods at least, he believes to be concrete.

His well-known repudiation of a materialistic world in which human values appear to be an intrusion defines negatively, in a rough way, the sort of concreteness he believes in. Speaking more positively, we may say that his standard of concreteness is the 'actual entity,' a being in whose 'concrescence' (or, in the case of God, in whose eternality) value is intrinsic, a being in whom alone all reasons why things are as they are must be found. This is his 'ontological principle,' and much of my criticism is directed towards showing that the ramifications of his system do not sustain it. But I should perhaps insist here that there is another tendency in Whitehead, not much discussed in the present work, that prepares the way for this ultimate diminution of the importance of the actual entity. That tendency I might sum up as Whitehead's nonmaterialistic atomism—that is, his tendency to find his model for actual entities (other than God) in what he calls 'electro-magnetic occasions.' Whitehead has himself introduced the image of Leibniz's monads to clarify what he means by an 'actual occasion,' but there is a vital difference between a Leibnizian monad and a Whiteheadian actual occasion. A monad, in Leibniz's view, can be understood as an entity (a genuine subject) correspondent to some minute physical happening, but it can also be understood as an entity (a genuine subject) correspondent to something as complex as a man. The monad "Alexander" or "Caesar" defines the being of Alexander or Caesar no less than some other monad might define (or correspond to) an electro-magnetic occasion. But there are no Whiteheadian monads or actual occasions that define something as complex as a man. The continuity of a man is, then, not that of an entity (or genuine subject) but that of a 'society.' It is a Leibnizian colony of monads but without its dominant monad.

No news, perhaps, to hear that in Whitehead's system a man can not have the status of an active and substantial *subject*. And if our only way of conceiving of the person as a subject were that of Leibniz, we might think of this as an advantage in Whitehead's system. But my point is that the reluctance to grant the status of entity (in the sense of an active substantial subject) to so complex a thing as a man is in Whitehead's case but a symptom of a general reluctance to regard *any* of his atomic actual occasions as active and substantial subjects. Whitehead of course calls all finite actual entities or actual occasions 'subject-superjects,' and places a clear emphasis on the term 'superject.' It is the purpose of much of my criticism to show *a)* how extreme that emphasis is, and how poorly it sorts with the stress Whitehead wishes to lay on such conceptions as 'self-causation,' 'self-creation,' 'creativity' (or the creativity *of* an actual entity), and even 'feeling'; and *b)* how it is correlated with a marked tendency to endow 'eternal objects'—Whitehead's version of Platonic forms—with many of the traditional marks of substantiality, including even that of power.

There is one last sense in which the present essay is modest in scope. It is, in effect, a close reading of *Process and Reality,* and no attempt has been made to survey the now fairly substantial body of writing on Whitehead's work. But where other interpretations are different from my own, at least in emphasis, I do discuss what seemed to me the chief differences. Thus some reference is made to

William A. Christian's *An Interpretation of Whitehead's Metaphysics* (New Haven: Yale University Press, 1959); to Ivor Leclerc's essay "Form and Actuality" in the book by several hands of which he is also editor, *The Relevance of Whitehead* (London: Allen and Unwin; New York: Macmillan, 1961); and to the 1936 letter from Whitehead to Charles Hartshorne, which is published for the first time in the volume by several hands edited by George L. Kline, *Alfred North Whitehead: Essays on his Philosophy* (Englewood Cliffs, New Jersey: Prentice Hall, 1963).

The very many passages from *Process and Reality* I have found it necessary to quote have all been compared with the "Corrigenda for *Process and Reality*," which appear in Kline's volume. As it turned out, the only typographical errors in the passages I quote appear in List I of the Corrigenda. This list is made up of errors in the Macmillan edition (which I use) that were corrected in the English (Cambridge) edition; they are accordingly set right without comment in this book.

The profusion of technical terms set off by single quotation marks in *Process and Reality* offers some difficulties for the expositor. They appear not only when Whitehead *mentions* his technical terms, but often enough when he *uses* them as well. It sometimes seems that he wishes to remind the reader, when a term makes an appearance in use after an absence, that it is indeed a technical term that he is contemplating, for the single quotation marks may signalize the first appearance in use in a new context and then be dropped in subsequent appearances. But Whitehead is anything but consistent about these matters. I have tried to follow what I take to be the least confusing procedure. *a*) All technical terms of Whitehead's appear in single quotations when mentioned; terms other than Whitehead's that are mentioned appear in double quotation marks. *b*) Occasional brief passages from Whitehead appear in double quotation marks when run in with my exposition rather than set off by indentation. *c*) Where a technical term from Whitehead is used rather than mentioned for the first time in this book, or for the first

time after a considerable absence, it is set off by single quotation marks, which are then dropped in further use of the
term. But all this is a statement of good intent, and I do
not pretend to have achieved complete consistency about
these matters.

Works of Alfred North Whitehead from which quotations are drawn are cited by abbreviations as follows.

Process and Reality: An Essay in Cosmology (New
York: The Macmillan Co., 1929. Copyright 1929 by The
Macmillan Company, renewed 1957 by Evelyn White-
head.) PR.

Science and the Modern World (New York: The Macmillan Co., 1925. Copyright 1925 by The Macmillan Company, renewed 1953 by Evelyn Whitehead.) SMW.

Adventure of Ideas (New York: The Macmillan Co.,
1933. Copyright 1933 by The Macmillan Company,
renewed 1961 by Evelyn Whitehead.) AI.

Quotations from these works are reprinted with permission of The Macmillan Company.

The pagination of the American edition of *Process and
Reality* differs from that of the English edition. The pagination of the original 1925 edition of *Science and the
Modern World,* which I use, differs from the reprints
issued by Macmillan in 1926 and later years.

Edward Pols

Bowdoin College
August 18, 1965

CONTENTS

Whitehead's Metaphysics

A Critical Examination

of *Process and Reality*

A General View

of the Doctrine of Process *&* Reality

OUR EXPOSITION and internal criticism of the metaphysical doctrine of *Process and Reality* will be organized around the topic of freedom, to my mind the most fruitful topic one can take for this purpose. In this chapter I shall state the doctrine roundly in order to give the whole sweep of Whitehead's philosophy as seen from this point of view.

It would be premature to try to define the term "freedom" at this point, since it is part of our business to ask whether it is given any completely consistent meaning. But one can make certain preliminary observations. Anyone who looks to Whitehead for a doctrine of, say, free will will find that Whitehead is concerned rather to state a theory of causation that does not do violence to the freedom he associates with all 'actual entities'[1] whatsoever. To be an actual entity is both to exhibit causal efficacy and to be free, and any human freedom must therefore exemplify this general principle. Our exposition logically begins then with actual entities.

Whitehead employs the term 'actual occasion' interchangeably with the term 'actual entity,' with the provi-

---

1. See the Preface for an explanation of the conventions governing the use of quotation marks in this book.

sion that the former always excludes God from its scope.[2] Because he describes an actual occasion as the "limiting type of an event with only one member" (PR, 113), it is clear that in discussing his doctrine of freedom we have to do with actual entities in a sense somewhat narrower than the word "entity" is usually given: we have in fact to do with one-member events and with God (since God is an actual entity).

Now it is plain that this is a very cryptic definition. This can not be entirely avoided at this stage, for this book as a whole is really an attempt to analyze just what Whitehead means by the term 'actual entity,' the analysis being directed towards the developing of the relation between the terms 'freedom,' 'cause,' and 'actual entity.' But a certain preliminary orientation is possible. Actual entities are, first of all, the ultimate units of the universe; all other types of existence are said to be derived by abstraction from them, and they are not themselves divisible into more ultimate entities or parts.[3] The one actual entity that is not a spatio-temporal one (I shall henceforth use Whitehead's term 'extensive' in place of "spatio-temporal") is God. His 'primordial nature' is described as an eternal and static 'valuation' of a realm of 'eternal objects,' by means of which this realm, understood as a realm of 'possibilities,' becomes relevant to the world of extensive actual entities. This world of extensive actual entities is neither complete nor completable: each actual occasion is a 'locus for the universe' (PR, 123) and each is succeeded by later loci or 'perspectives.' It is the function of God to initiate such loci out of the *'impasse'* presented by any given state of affairs, and then to 'persuade' or 'lure' it towards the highest possible intensity of 'feeling.' The notion 'feeling' will be developed at some length later.

2. PR, 135. The term 'actual occasion' is used when Whitehead wishes to stress the 'extensiveness' of an 'actual entity,' "the term 'actual occasion' is used synonymously with 'actual entity'; but chiefly when its character of extensiveness has some direct relevance to the discussion, either extensiveness in the form of temporal extensiveness, that is to say 'duration,' or extensiveness in the form of spatial extension, or in the more complete signification of spatio-

Extensive actual entities, or actual occasions, can be given an interpretation in terms of physical science. Since an actual occasion is a limiting type of event, with one member, it is perhaps best described by way of the notion 'event.' Most of the entities that have until recently been thought of as material particles are classified as events with more than one member: "For example, a molecule is a historic route of actual occasions; and such a route is an 'event' " (PR, 124). But it is quite clear that one must go well below the order of a molecule to arrive at an actual occasion: even an electron is thought of as a 'route,' or 'society' of actual occasions (PR, 150). The prototype of the actual occasion in the world of physics is the indivisible 'electro-magnetic occasion,' which contributes to a society. In the realm of physics the hypothesis of such occasions is verified in so far as they help to make the experimental picture clearer, but they are inaccessible to even the indirect kind of observation that electrons can now be brought under. Their major characteristic is perhaps expressed in the notion that the development of such an occasion is not in physical time, although it can be spoken of as duration: physical time is a result of the togetherness of actual occasions, and is therefore, although a continuum to the observer, atomic in its growth. This is the 'epochal' theory of time, which will be discussed in more detail later.[4] Its corollary here is that an actual occasion, although it 'perishes,' neither changes nor moves: each 'enjoys' a quantum of space and time, but does not develop *in* it. The definition of change is given as follows.

> The most general sense of the meaning of change is 'the differences between actual occasions in one event.' . . . Now the motion of the molecule is nothing else than the

temporal extensiveness" (PR, 119). It is, however, important to note that he is not always completely consistent, and sometimes uses 'actual occasion' in a context where its scope should include God, e.g., PR, 113.

3. This is a statement of the 'ontological principle'; it is contended in chapters 5 and 6 that Whitehead's doctrine of 'eternal objects' makes for quite a different picture of reality.

4. See chapter 2, section C1.

differences between the successive occasions of its life-history in respect to the extensive quanta from which they arise; and the changes in the molecule are the consequential differences in the actual occasions (PR, 124–25).

And the actual occasion, which does not change, is the "outcome of whatever can be ascribed to it in the way of quality or relationship" (PR, 122). It has no 'external adventures' but only the 'internal adventure' of becoming (PR, 124). Whitehead's view of change is of course ultimately Platonic in the sense that " 'Change' is the description of the adventures of eternal objects, i.e. forms, in the evolving universe of actual things," [5] and reality properly to be described as a 'flux of forms.' [6]

Two cautions are perhaps in order before we proceed with the theme of freedom. The first concerns the restricted sense in which the terms 'actual entity' and 'actual occasion' are employed by Whitehead; the second concerns a too facile identification of eternal objects and Platonic forms.

As to the first, we cannot give any concrete examples of actual entities. And this leads at once to a paradox that bears stressing. Whitehead often calls his philosophy a philosophy of organism, and he tells us that we must think of the activity of actual entities in terms of such organic categories as aim and feeling. Yet nothing that is an organism in the ordinary sense of that word qualifies as an example of an actual entity. Organisms are in fact *societies* of actual entities. Those who seek comfort in the humanistic tone of Whitehead's philosophy had best, therefore, be aware that his metaphysics offers many difficulties for a theory of the person. A man, like other organisms, is a society of actual entities. And Whitehead is consistent about this until the end. In *Modes of Thought,* which is of course a late work, he speaks of man as an 'aggregation of actualities.' Man is, to be sure, the highest

5. PR, 92; cf. PR, 44. In chapters 5 and 6 the relation of this view of 'forms' to the problem of the substantiality and freedom of 'actual entities' is discussed at length.

6. PR, 74, *passim.*

of the four types of aggregations Whitehead recognizes there,[7] but he is no less a 'social aggregation' of actual entities for all that. We have not, therefore, a doctrine of a hierarchy of entities as in the cases of Aristotelian *ousiai* or Leibnizian monads. The familiar traditional notion that man is a higher *kind of entity* is replaced by the notion that within the society which is a man an especially high *kind of event* (consciousness, choice, abstract thought, etc.) occurs. The obvious parallels with Leibniz's doctrine make it especially important to stress the differences between his doctrine and Whitehead's. For a Leibniz confronted with today's science, we may suppose, an electro-magnetic occasion, an atom, a molecule, a living cell, a man, would all of them qualify as monads; but for Whitehead, despite the superficial resemblance between the categories "monad" and 'actual entity,' only the first of the list would qualify as an actual entity.

As to the second caution, Whitehead often calls the eternal objects Platonic forms, but he is careful to point out some differences between the two notions as well. In Whitehead's doctrine eternal objects are said to 'ingress' in actual entities, while Plato would maintain that actual entities participate in the forms. The difference in terminology marks a real difference of intent. Thus, while eternal objects are transcendent in the sense that one of them may ingress in many actual entities, they are, on the other hand, meant precisely for that role of ingression. They do not lead another life of which their ingression in actuality is but a reminder. They are possibilities, but only by being forms of definiteness *of* actual entities, and thus can not have another and ideal state of being over against which the definiteness of actual entities is somehow deficient. We shall in the course of this work question whether Whitehead is successful in maintaining the coeval status of actual entities and eternal objects that his principle of coherence makes necessary. But there is no doubt about his intent.

7. Alfred North Whitehead, *Modes of Thought* (New York: Macmillan, 1938), pp. 38–39.

From this it follows also that as forms of definiteness the eternal objects constitute a democracy: for every shade of definiteness of actuality there is an eternal object furnishing that definiteness by its ingression. The doubts Socrates expresses in the *Parmenides* do not therefore arise, and there is indeed an eternal object corresponding to each mean and deplorable shade of definiteness no less than to what is noble and elevated. Eternal objects consequently do not form a realm except as God (considered in his 'primordial' nature) makes them by his 'envisagement' or 'valuation' into an ordered ideal for the whole of actuality. William A. Christian in his *An Interpretation of Whitehead's Metaphysics* gives a useful inventory of the types of eternal objects that Whitehead mentions as such.[8] Among the items are: 'sensa,' such as definite shades of color; subjective qualities, such as emotions or other affective tones; mathematical universals, such as triplicity; logical notions, such as 'any'; and forms of imperfection. Yet there are certain difficulties about citing clear-cut examples of eternal objects, despite their ubiquity and despite the plenitude of examples Whitehead gives. The difficulties arise chiefly from the distinction Whitehead makes between the individual essence and the relational essence of eternal objects, but we shall defer detailed consideration of them until chapter 6, and return now to the topic of freedom.

In this book the doctrine of freedom will in the main be taken as concerning extensive actual entities, or actual occasions. God will, however, appear as the standard of freedom, and there will be some occasion to speak of the sense in which he too is free.

Freedom, then, is thought of as a possession of actual entities, which may have it in degrees ranging upward from the negligible. One would perhaps be better advised to say that the notion 'freedom' is an ingredient of the

8. William A. Christian, *An Interpretation of Whitehead's Metaphysics* (New Haven: Yale University Press, 1959), pp. 202–3. Christian's list should be consulted; to rehearse it in detail at this point would confuse matters as some items in it are not explained until later in the present work.

notion 'actual entity'; but one must then hasten to add that another ingredient is the notion 'condition.' All these notions, however, go to form what is essentially a theory of causation,[9] for one of Whitehead's primary purposes appears to be the avoidance of any way of speech that would oppose freedom and causation. An actual entity is described as both caused, and as itself originative of causal efficacy; and freedom is often enough identified with 'self-causation.' When Whitehead so expresses himself, one would not be far wrong in identifying the factor of condition in an actual entity with efficient causation, and the factor of freedom with final causation, where 'efficient cause' means 'datum for feeling' and 'final cause' means "the 'how' of the feeling."

> Thus the feeling would be wrongly abstracted from its own final cause. This final cause is an inherent element in the feeling, constituting the unity of that feeling. An actual entity feels as it does feel in order to be the actual entity which it is. In this way an actual entity satisfies Spinoza's notion of substance: it is *causa sui* (PR, 339).[10]

It is unfortunate that the account cannot be entirely clear at this point without anticipating the discussion of the idea of 'feeling' in chapter 2. But a sketch of the idea of 'feeling' may be helpful at this point. Whitehead intends the idea to be an ultimate, in the sense that an actual entity is said to be a 'real togetherness' of other actual entities, and the real togetherness is thought of as 'togetherness in a feeling.' It is important to note that there is no feeler apart from the togetherness which is the feeling. The regress of internal relations which such a doctrine seems to imply, and to which exception is frequently taken by students of Whitehead, is denied by Whitehead in his doctrine of 'eternal objects' of the 'objective' species,[11] which enables him to assert that the whole

---

9. "Causation is nothing else than one outcome of the principle that every actual entity has to house *its* actual world" (PR, 124).
10. See chapter 2, section B.
11. This may indeed break the regress of internal relations, but, if it does, it does so by means of giving 'eternal objects' a kind of

content of an actual entity is not given by the subjectivity of its feelings. The contention—which we may here treat in a nontechnical way—is that the 'data' felt are not *all* of them feelings, and that this objective character of what is felt is transmitted by the new actual entity, so that it itself, as a datum for future actual entities, is not constituted wholly by feelings.

Returning now to the topic of causation, we may observe that the terms 'causation,' 'freedom,' 'actual entity,' and 'feeling' can none of them be abstracted from the others, and that causation is a complex matter involving at least an efficient cause or condition, and a final cause, or freedom factor, or factor of self-causation.[12]

But the account is still incomplete in that freedom could still be construed as exhausted between an actual entity's freedom *from* complete conformity to, or repetition of, the conditions it is confronted with, and its freedom *for* the determinations which a final cause might effect. On such an account Whitehead would, to be sure, avoid what Bergson calls radical mechanism.

> The essence of mechanical explanation, in fact, is to regard the future and the past as calculable functions of the present, and thus to claim that *all is given*.[13]

> Radical mechanism implies a metaphysic in which the totality of the real is postulated complete in eternity, and in which the apparent duration of things expresses merely the infirmity of a mind that cannot know everything at once.[14]

But he would avoid it only at the expense of falling into a radical finalism, which

> substitutes the attraction of the future for the impulsion of the past. But succession remains none the less a mere appearance, as indeed does movement itself.[15]

ultimate status. It will be contended in the course of this essay that the whole of the 'feeling'—both its 'data,' and its 'how,' or subjective character—is nothing more than a certain kind of configuration, or togetherness, of eternal objects, both of the 'objective' and of the 'subjective' species.

12. For another comment on an entity as *causa sui,* see PR, 135.

The explicit side of Whitehead's doctrine of freedom repudiates both radical finalism and radical mechanism. An actual entity is conditioned by the actual world,[16] but it is in a sense free from it; *freedom for* does not however necessarily take away what *freedom from* confers. The freedom factor, or factor of self-causation, is indeed identified with final causation, but this latter term is used to designate something that is a 'lure,' or 'persuasion,' rather than a determinant. Much of Whitehead's discussion of freedom is given in such metaphorical terms. His point here is that in order for the realm of 'possibility' to present genuine alternatives—by which alone it would deserve the name of the realm of *possibility*—it must be thought of as containing lures, rather than compulsive configurations of eternal objects which would determine the future of an actual entity confronted with such pseudopossibilities.

As will be noticed in more detail later, it is God, in his primordial nature, who gives the realm of eternal objects the kind of relevance to the world of actual entities that makes it a genuine realm of possibilities, or lures for feeling. This nondeterminative role of God's primordial nature is implicit in the conception of 'initial subjective aim,' which expresses one side of God's relation to other actual entities. An actual entity is a growing together or 'concrescence' of feelings; among these feelings there is one called the 'subjective aim,' which gives the concrescence unity and guides its development. Since God is the 'principle of concretion,' which gives an actual entity its start, he must give it an initial subjective aim, in virtue of which it is first constituted as a 'concrescence of feelings.'

> an originality in the temporal world is conditioned, though not determined, by an initial subjective aim supplied by the ground of all order and of all originality (PR, 164).

13. Henri Bergson, *Creative Evolution*, tr. Arthur Mitchell (New York: Henry Holt & Co., 1913), p. 37.
14. *Ibid.*, p. 39.
15. *Ibid.*, p. 39.
16. The settled, determinate world which the growth of the 'feeling' of a new 'actual entity' must in some respects conform to.

In this sense God is the principle of concretion; namely, he is that actual entity from which each temporal concrescence receives that initial aim *from which its self-causation starts.* That aim determines the initial gradation of relevance of eternal objects for conceptual feeling; and constitutes *the autonomous subject* in its primary phase of feelings with its initial conceptual valuations, and with its initial physical purposes. . . .

If we prefer the phraseology, we can say that God and the actual world jointly constitute the character of the creativity for the initial phase of the novel concrescence. *The subject, thus constituted, is the autonomous master of its own concrescence into subject-superject* (PR, 374, italics supplied).

It was the idea of the final cause as a determinate essence, nature, eternal object, or Platonic form ordaining what the future of some entity would be that caused Bergson to bring the charge of radical finalism against certain metaphysical systems. If it were not for the insistence on defining final causation in terms of a lure, or persuasion, as we have just noticed, one might have made the summary decision that Whitehead's theory was open to the same charge. But despite the qualifications, which as we have so far seen them are given in terms of initial subjective aim, there remains a problem concerning subjective aim as a whole and not just in its initial phase. For subjective aim seems, at any moment, to be a perfectly *determinate* component of an entity, even though it is made equivalent to self-causation (or self-creation) and final causation.

Whitehead specifically identifies 'self-causation' and 'final causation'; [17] and he also identifies 'subjective aim' with 'final causation' [18] so that one would expect 'self-causation' and 'subjective aim' to be identified, and this is

17. See the passage on PR, 339, which is quoted earlier; also PR, 338.
18. The following passages are of interest. "concrescence moves toward its final cause, which is its subjective aim . . ." (PR, 320). "The subject-superject is the purpose of the process originating the feelings. The feelings are inseparable from the end at which they aim; and this end is the feeler. The feelings aim at the feeler, as

in fact done at several points.[19] There is moreover good enough warrant throughout *Process and Reality* for the equivalence of the three terms with the factor of freedom. But subjective aim seems, at least occasionally, to be taken as a determinate component, and as belonging therefore to the realm of condition, or efficient causation, as in the following passage, where it seems rather opposed to than allied with, or identical with, a free self-creation.

> The doctrine of the philosophy of organism is that, however far the sphere of efficient causation be pushed in the determination of components of a concrescence—its data, its emotions, its appreciations, *its purposes, its phases of subjective aim*—beyond the determination of these components there always remains the final reaction of the universe. This final reaction completes the self-creative act by putting the decisive stamp of creative emphasis upon the determinations of efficient cause. Each occasion exhibits its measure of creative emphasis in proportion to its measure of subjective intensity (PR, 75; italics supplied).

Whitehead may of course intend this restriction to apply only to initial subjective aim; or, in speaking of the 'phases of subjective aim,' he may be thinking of what the subjective aim has been at various times in the entity's past, rather than what it is at a present moment from which a decision is to issue. It is not to be expected that this difficulty can be cleared up at this stage. The matter will perhaps be somewhat clearer after the discussion of the 'modification' of subjective aim in chapter 3. However this may be, the present passage decisively expresses Whitehead's wish to avoid both radical mechanism and radical finalism; for the sense in which subjective aim might be a component furnishing a determination is the sense in

their final cause" (PR, 339). "In this way the decision derived from the actual world, which is the efficient cause, is completed by the decision embodied in the subjective aim which is the final cause" (PR, 423). See also PR 159, 340, etc.

19. For instance, "The concrescence is dominated by a subjective aim which essentially concerns the creature as a final superject. The subjective aim is this subject itself determining its own self-creation as one creature" (PR, 108).

which the theory might lean towards radical finalism. This is all that we are concerned with at this point. The positive factor by which the radical finalism is avoided is the notion of the 'final reaction of the self-creative unity of the universe,' which appears elsewhere in other guises. Thus the ninth Categoreal Obligation puts it in the following form.

> *The Category of Freedom and Determination.*
> The concrescence of each individual actual entity is internally determined and externally free.
> This category can be condensed into the formula, that in each concrescence whatever is determinable is determined, but that there is always a remainder for the decision of the subject-superject of that concrescence. This subject-superject is the universe in that synthesis, and beyond it there is nonentity. This final decision is the reaction of the unity of the whole to its own internal determination. This reaction is the final modification of emotion, appreciation, and purpose. But the decision of the whole arises out of the determination of the parts, so as to be strictly relevant to it (PR, 41–42).

There will be occasion to return again and again to this notion of the 'final reaction of the self-creative unity of the universe.' It is here important that this final reaction occurs in the concrescence of feelings that is an actual entity, or, in the present case, a 'subject-superject.' The term 'subject' here reflects the insistence that this final reaction occurs within an entity that feels—for the notion of feeling requires the notion of subjectivity; the term 'superject' adds the qualification that the feeler is not something over and above its feelings, and the qualification amounts to an assertion that subjectivity does not require a subject in the sense of a substantial entity that might *have* feelings. The problem of the subject-superject will be dealt with later, particularly in chapter 4; it is introduced here in order to characterize further the actual entity in which the final reaction of the self-creative unity of the universe is said to take place.

This whole doctrine, the theory of the reaction of the self-creative unity of the universe; the formula that everything that is determinable is determined, but that not everything is determined; the identification of 'subjective aim,' 'final causation,' and 'self-causation' (with the confusing reservation in respect of 'subjective aim' that seems designed to avoid radical finalism);—this whole doctrine has as its corollary the characterization of God's ordering activity as a persuasion, rather than a compulsion, which we have already noticed in passing.

> The sheer force of things lies in the intermediate physical process: this is the energy of physical production. God's role is not the combat of productive force with productive force, of destructive force with destructive force; it lies in the patient operation of the overpowering rationality of his conceptual harmonization (PR, 525–26).

> He is the lure for feeling, the eternal urge of desire. His particular relevance to each creative act as it arises from its own conditioned standpoint in the world, constitutes him the initial 'object of desire' establishing the initial phase of each subjective aim (PR, 522).

The sense of this corollary is simply that the notion of an entity as free, if it is coupled with the idea of the existence, or subsistence, of a realm of possibilities, requires that this realm be so described as actually to offer genuine alternatives. Here the initial subjective aim constitutes the actual entity in a certain way, but does not tell the whole story of the entity's final state; nor does the character of the realm of possibility tell the whole of this story—and this is the significance of the terms 'lure' and 'persuasion.' There are considerable difficulties in Whitehead's use of these terms, but discussion of them will be deferred until chapter 3.[20]

20. Some preliminary survey of these ambiguities may be useful at this point. God, having constituted an actual entity with an 'initial subjective aim,' is not strictly speaking a 'lure,' in respect of that initial aim. There are two senses in which he can be a lure, of which the first is not tenable. *a*) Before the initial subjective aim emerges (and therefore before the new actual entity emerges), he can be

Any actual entity, then, is *a) caused* by the other actual entities that are fully determinate at its inception, in so far as it is what it is because of what these other actual entities are. As a 'growing together' of feelings, it must feel just these entities, or rather, elements from them. This is what Whitehead calls efficient causation, and what I shall refer to as the *factor of condition.* And every actual entity is *b)* itself a cause of its own development in that it is its own reason for just how [21] it will incorporate into itself, or feel, those elements it must feel (its 'objectified world'),[22] because of its initial subjective aim, from each of the determinate actual entities given to it (its 'actual world'). This is the factor of self-causation, or as I shall say, the *factor of freedom,* and it represents an attempt to preserve a sense in which an entity is free, while every component in its history is caused. Thus both the factor of condition and the factor of freedom are *causal* factors, where "causal" would mean "sources of the determinateness that an entity has when its history is over." This *explicit* doctrine is a pluralism in the sense that any actual entity makes a contribution of its own to the total of

thought of as luring a certain complex of feelings, with its unifying feeling, or initial subjective aim, out of a settled state of affairs. And this interpretation is supported by the fact that the initial subjective aim is a certain kind of feeling of God's 'primordial nature.' But God brings the best (at least initially) out of any settled state of affairs—and this seems to make his function anything but a luring, for God simply determines the initial status of the new actual entity. *b)* The actual entity, once constituted, with its initial subjective aim, has genuine alternatives open to it. By the 'ontological principle' these alternatives, or 'possibilities,' are in God's primordial nature. As we have observed in a preliminary fashion, he makes the realm of eternal objects relevant to, but not compulsive in respect of, the new actual entity. This is the sense—and the only acceptable one, I think—in which he is a lure; and it is merely the sense in which he offers, or contains, genuine possibilities to a partially free actual entity.

21. The sense "how" as in the present context involves considerations that cannot be made clear until chapter 2. Provisionally it can be said that the definiteness of a felt actual entity *A* is the definiteness of a real togetherness of a selection of eternal objects. Some of these eternal objects are of such a type ('objective species') that they can only be data for the feeling of a new actual entity *B.* Others are of a different sort ('subjective species') and can **both**

actuality. I have noticed before that the account of 'actual entity' is an account of both 'freedom' and 'cause'; it can now be added (omitting God from our scope) that any actual entity *a)* is in part caused by the efficient causes represented by its objectified world; *b)* is in part self-caused, or a "free cause" of its own development; and *c)* is itself an efficient cause, in that it forms part of the objectified world of subsequent actual entities. The whole account could be of course extended to God if it were advisable to consider at this point his 'consequent nature.'

Besides the Category of Freedom and Determination, which has already been mentioned, the interdependence of the terms 'condition,' 'cause,' 'actual entity,' and 'freedom' presupposes two other categories. The fourth of the Categories of Explanation embodies the 'principle of relativity.'

> *iv*] That the potentiality for being an element in a real concrescence of many entities into one actuality, is the one general metaphysical character attaching to all entities, actual and non-actual; and that every item in its universe is involved in each concrescence. In other words, it belongs

characterize the internality of the felt actual entity *A,* i.e. *its* feelings of earlier entities, and act as data for the feelings of *B.* Eternal objects of this latter type can also be repeated in *B* as part of the pattern of the internality of its feeling. Now the how of a feeling is given entirely by the eternal objects characterizing its internality, with the qualification (however obscure) that the configuration of eternal objects is always configuration in a feeling. The present point is that the actual entity *B* is partly responsible for the how of its feelings, because it joins eternal objects selected from the realm of possibility (as in God's 'primordial nature'), with eternal objects derived from *A,* to form the full internality of its feelings. The validity of this conception is challenged at many points in this the present book.

22. "The term 'objectification' refers to the particular mode in which the potentiality of one actual entity is realized in another actual entity" (PR, 34). "The functioning of one actual entity in the self-creation of another actual entity is the 'objectification' of the former for the latter actual entity" (PR, 38). The total of such objectifications constitutes the 'objectified world' of an 'actual entity.' The distinction between 'actual world' and 'objectification' is given in greater detail in chapter 2, section B.

to the nature of a 'being' that it is a potential for every 'becoming.' This is the 'principle of relativity' (PR, 33).[23]

This is one way of asserting that process is at the heart of Whitehead's system. It is his fundamental tenet that the universe is neither complete nor completable, and the principle of relativity merely expresses this fact from the point of view of a completed entity taken as material for a further progress. The idea of creativity, on the other hand, embodies the notion of the activity that utilizes such material. The Category of the Ultimate states how the notion of creativity, the final reaction of the self-creative unity of the universe, is bound up with the interdependent terms under discussion.

'Creativity,' 'many,' 'one' are the ultimate notions involved in the meaning of the synonymous terms 'thing,' 'being,' 'entity.' These three notions complete the Category of the Ultimate and are presupposed in all the more special categories.

The term 'one' does not stand for 'the integral number *one*,' which is a complex special notion. . . . It stands for the singularity of an entity. The term 'many' presupposes the term 'one,' and the term 'one' presupposes the term 'many.' The term 'many' conveys the notion of 'disjunctive diversity.' . . . There are many 'beings' in disjunctive diversity.

'Creativity' is the universal of universals characterizing ultimate matter of fact. It is the ultimate principle by which the many, which are the universe disjunctively, become the one actual occasion, which is the universe conjunctively. It lies in the nature of things that the many enter into complex unity.

'Creativity' is the principle of *novelty*. An actual occa-

23. The other side of the principle of relativity is that each entity in some sense requires all other entities. Whitehead denies that *any* entity can be free in the sense of Spinoza's definition: "a thing is called free which exists from the necessity of its own nature alone, and is determined to action by itself alone" (Def. VII, *Ethic*, First Part). A fundamental fact is the coherence of the universe, and Whitehead demands that a metaphysical system reflect this coherence. This is one of the reasons for his rejection of a God with "eminent" reality.

sion is a novel entity diverse from any entity in the 'many' which it unifies. . . . The 'creative advance' is the application of this ultimate principle of creativity to each novel situation which it originates (PR, 31–32).

A summary account of the relation of the two notions 'entity' and 'freedom' might run as follows: on the one hand each actual entity is in *some* ways free—and this means that extensive actual entities are in some ways free both from one another and from God, and God (in his primordial nature) free from extensive actual entities. On the other hand, each actual entity is in some sense conditioned—and this means that extensive actual entities are *not completely* free from each other and from God, and God (now in his consequent nature) [24] not completely free from extensive actual entities.

There are no actual entities, therefore, that do not in *some* measure meet Spinoza's criterion for substance, namely, that it should exist "from the necessity of its own nature." It is only *components* of an entity that are *completely* determined [25]—a principle that is the obverse of the ontological principle, which asserts that all reasons must be found in some actual entity or other. The determinateness of components, by the way, and the determinateness of their relations one to another, gives the sense in which "everything that is determinable is determined," or alternatively, the sense in which there appears no arbitrary break in the causal sequence that forms a thing's *past*. Both Bergson and Whitehead have noticed the sense in which the history of any entity can be viewed as a succession of efficiently causal connections. Thus Bergson:

24. In his 'consequent nature,' (see PR, 523–25; 531–33, *passim* as indexed) God 'feels' other 'actual entities,' as he does not do in his 'primordial nature.' It is one expression of Whitehead's principle of coherence, that God is 'deficiently actual' in the side of his nature that is abstracted from his feelings of other actual entities. The principle of coherence simply states that any actual entity, *qua* actual, must feel, in some way, all other actual entities.

25. This does not mean that *all* components of an entity are so determined, rather "every component *which is determinable* is internally determined" (PR, 75; italics supplied).

For each of our acts we shall easily find antecedents of which it may in some sort be said to be the mechanical resultant. And it may equally well be said that each action is the realization of an intention. In this sense mechanism is everywhere, and finality everywhere, in the evolution of our conduct. But if our action be one that involves the whole of our person and is truly ours, it could not have been foreseen, even though its antecedents explain it when once it has been accomplished. And though it be the realizing of an intention, it differs, as a *present* and *new* reality, from the intention which can never aim at anything but recommencing or rearranging the past.[26]

And Whitehead writes in a similar vein.

The evolution of history can be rationalized by the consideration of the determination of successors by antecedents. But, on the other hand, the evolution of history is incapable of rationalization because it exhibits a selected flux of participating forms. No reason, internal to history, can be assigned why that flux of forms, rather than another flux, should have been illustrated. It is true that any flux must exhibit the character of internal determination. So much follows from the ontological principle. But every instance of internal determination assumes *that* flux up to *that* point. There is no reason why there could be no alternative flux exhibiting that principle of internal determination. The actual flux presents itself with the character of being merely 'given' (PR, 74).

Both Bergson and Whitehead are concerned here with the point that determinations are always observable in any history and that such determinations need not determine what a future history will contain. Determination, in this restricted sense, is irrelevant to freedom: *any* history, or *any* complex will reveal a connectedness of elements if we consider what is already given; and in this respect a deterministic world and one containing freedom would appear the same to the backward view. There are, however, special difficulties posed by Whitehead's doctrine of subjective aim and by his conception of the role of God's

26. *Op. cit.,* p. 47.

primordial nature. These difficulties are dealt with in some detail in chapter 3.

It appears, then, that there are several elements in what I have called the factor of freedom: *a)* indetermination; *b)* as a correlate of the indetermination, novelty, which, reflecting perhaps an optimistic bias, is sometimes identified with creative *advance;* *c)* self-causation [27] (or self-creation) in the sense of an aim at a certain 'subjective intensity' of feeling. The first element is a negative one, which asserts merely that the determinate components of an actual entity taken at any one phase do not determine wholly the next phase. The second suggests that because the future is not contained in the past, the future is genuinely new, in respect of the extensive world, at any rate. And the third element is not only necessary to the theory in general, but is also intended to answer the very important question "*What* is free?" 'Intensity' here means the measure of the multiplicity of components that "can enter explicit feelings as contrasts," without being "dismissed into negative prehensions as incompatibilities." [28] And the word "certain" in (*c*) refers to the fact that the intensity aimed at is limited, but not decided, by the factor of condition; and also to the fact that the intensity aimed at is not necessarily identical with the *maximum* permitted by the factor of condition.[29] The

27. The following passage is of interest here. "To be *causa sui* means that the process of concrescence is its own reason for the decision in respect to the qualitative clothing of feelings. It is finally responsible for the decision by which any lure for feeling is admitted to efficiency. *The freedom inherent in the universe is constituted by this element of self-causation*" (PR, 135; italics supplied).

28. PR, 128. It seems best to defer for the moment any further consideration of 'contrasts,' as this matter will be clearer after the doctrine of feeling has been further developed. 'Contrasts' will be discussed again in chapter 2, where they are of importance in connection with the problem of 'intensity.'

29. The following passage, however, is an interesting comment on the underlying optimism of Whitehead. The new actuality, or novel fact, mentioned in the passage does not exact the maximum from the conditions ('society') out of which it springs, because of the fact that the society is the "wrong" one, "the novel fact may throw back, inhibit, and delay. But the advance, when it does arrive, will be richer in content, more fully conditioned, and more stable. For in its

creative purpose in general (which includes God's subjective aim) is "that each unification [of the universe] shall
achieve some maximum depth of intensity of feeling, subject to the conditions of its concrescence" (PR, 381). But
from the point of view of an extensive actual entity, the
'creative purpose in general,' where that purpose includes
God's purpose but excludes its own purpose, belongs to
the factor of condition rather than to the factor of freedom.[30]

It is interesting to observe that though the aim of any
extensive actual entity does not necessarily result in the
highest degree of subjective intensity available to it on the
basis of the conditions out of which it grows, Whitehead
nevertheless tends to equate degree of freedom with the
degree of intensity that is actually chosen.

> beyond the determination of these components there al-
> ways remains the final reaction of the self-creative unity of
> the universe. This final reaction completes the self-
> creative act by putting the decisive stamp of creative
> emphasis upon the determinations of efficient cause. *Each
> occasion exhibits its measure of creative emphasis in pro-
> portion to its measure of subjective intensity.* The absolute
> standard of such intensity is that of the primordial nature
> of God . . . (PR, 75; italics supplied).

My contention is true if, as I think we may, we take
'measure of creative emphasis' to be identical with 'degree
of freedom.' There is a certain logic to this, for the less
subjective intensity an actual entity chooses, within the
scope offered by its conditions, the more those conditions
are permitted to bear in upon it, and the more, therefore,
it can be thought of as *conforming* to them or as subject to
their efficient causation.

Although the three elements of freedom are perhaps

objective efficacy an actual entity can only inhibit by reason of its
alternative positive contribution" (PR, 341).
30. This of course is dependent upon Whitehead's theory that the
initial subjective aim, which is given by God, and which is the *best*
for that actual entity, in that it is an aim at maximum intensity, is
not identical with what I might venture to call the "final" subjective
aim. This theory is questioned in chapter 3.

not consistent with all of Whitehead's remarks on this subject, they represent a reasonably accurate scheme of his theory of freedom. Some of the difficulties that reside in the relations between the terms 'conformation,' 'subjective intensity,' and 'degree of freedom' will be dealt with later.

2

The Doctrine in detail

Factor of Freedom & Factor of Condition

Introduction

THIS CHAPTER will be devoted mainly to an expository discussion of what I have called the *factor of freedom* and the *factor of condition*. The exposition will be carried out by means of several pairs of complementary terms, each of which embodies in one fashion or another this fundamental contrast.

A] *mental pole, conceptual feelings |*
                   physical pole, physical feelings.
B] *subjective aim | objectification.*
C] *novelty, creative advance, intensity |*
                   conformation, reproduction.
D] *subjective form | datum for feeling.*
E] *objective lure, lure for feeling, real potentiality |*
                   actual world, the given.

One or more sections of the chapter will be devoted to each of these contrasts.

    It must be plain at once that there is something arbitrary about the choice of just these terms, and also that the character of their opposition is not always precisely analogous. Moreover, some of the terms are broader than others—'mental pole,' for instance, includes 'subjective aim'—with the consequence that there will be some repetition. But all of the notions to be developed here will reappear in the succeeding more critical chapters, and it therefore seems desirable to introduce them in this place. Some of the more important difficulties noticed will be treated rather summarily at this point, their more thorough elucidation being reserved for the following critical chapters. I hope, however, that the discussion will serve as an outline of some of the more important ideas in Whitehead's metaphysics. Accordingly, such basic ideas as 'actual entity,' 'prehension,' 'feeling,' 'eternal object,' 'God's primordial nature,' etc., will be introduced as they become necessary to the understanding of our several complementary contrasts. The sense in which the concrescence of an actual entity is describable in terms of feeling will be important throughout our exposition. Indeed, the doctrine of an entity as a concrescence, or growing together of feelings, or prehensions, together with the doctrine of eternal objects, form the whole background of our examination of *Process and Reality* in terms of the problem of freedom.

A.

'Mental pole', 'conceptual feelings' |
'physical pole', 'physical feelings'

I.

WHITEHEAD ON THE RELATIONS BETWEEN ACTUAL ENTITIES

The terms 'mental pole' and 'physical pole' are so wide as to be roughly equivalent to what I have called the factor of freedom and the factor of condition respectively. The physical pole represents the totality of actual entities by which a given new actual entity is conditioned, in accordance with the general requirement of the Category of the Ultimate that "the many, which are the universe disjunctively, become the one actual occasion, which is the universe conjunctively" (PR, 31). It is necessary to explain Whitehead's views on how one entity conditions another before the correlate activity of the mental pole can be made clear. But first a sketch of Whitehead's views on the relations between actual entities is in order.

Whitehead's theory of relations has two sides, the one concerning the relations between actual entities, the other concerning the relations between eternal objects, or abstract entities. The two senses are interrelated in that the character of an actual entity is always the character of a certain togetherness of eternal objects; but at this point we shall be concerned only with the relations between actual entities, reserving the other problem for chapters 5 and 6. Although there are certain reservations, which I shall notice shortly, the relation between any member of the group of settled and complete actual entities that form the 'actual world' of a new actual entity and that new actual entity is a relation with only one genuine term. Here I use the term "genuine," in a sense accordant with A. C. Ewing's claim that "no tolerable view of relations can be incompatible with the fact that the same term may stand in different relations," and his further conclusion that "it cannot be true that all relations alter or modify their terms, if by this is meant that they cause a change in their terms." [1] The point is that the new actual entity cannot meet these requirements in respect of any of its relations to the actual entities that form its actual world, while any of these felt actual entities does meet these requirements in respect of the new actual entity. The new actual entity feels its actual world, but it is wholly constituted by these feelings, together with its feelings of the realm of eternal objects. The fundamental feature of the internal relations of an actual entity to other actual entities is, then, that they are feelings, where the feeler in question is simply the unity of its feelings (in a sense that is yet to be examined).

There is, however, a reservation. It has already been noticed that Whitehead avoids a regress of internal relations by the doctrine of eternal objects of the objective species, which, though they qualify an entity, do not do so

1. A. C. Ewing, *Idealism: A Critical Survey* (New York: Humanities Press, 1934), pp. 125–26.

as an element in the subjectivity of its feelings. In the internal relation that is a feeling, what is felt is always an actual entity that is not reducible to *its* feelings, so that the felt actual entity is given a status that allows it to be externally related (in the sense referred to above as genuine) to the new actual entity that feels it. It will be observed that if this were not the case there would be a regress of internal relations, and hence no external relations at all.

Now it is because of this status of the felt entities that the new actual entity is given a status as a term in the relation. It may not be the status of a genuine term, in the sense given above, if we consider only its relations to the entities it feels, but it is at least the status of something "outside" or "other than" the entities felt. The new actual entity, although it is constituted by its feelings, can be "other than" the data of those feelings, only if those data themselves are capable of external relations. The character of the new actual entity is such as to give it an extensive status (a space-time 'region') distinct from that of any of its predecessors, although completely given by the feelings it has of those predecessors. The part the *felt* actual entities play here is dependent on the fact that eternal objects of the objective species "are the mathematical Platonic forms" (PR, 446), and as such "express the theory of extension in its most general aspect" (PR, 448). Because eternal objects of this sort form part of the *data* of the feelings of the new actual entity, it bears along in its development its reference to them, which reference is modified by its own feelings of the realm of eternal objects, and is left behind it after its concrescence as *its* irreducible objectivity, part of which expresses its place in the extensive world.

On the doctrine of self-causation, the part an actual entity's feeling of the realm of eternal objects plays cannot be minimized: just as its extensive region depends on its internal relations to the eternal objects of the objective species that characterize the entities it feels, so does its own subjectivity depend on its internal relations to the eternal objects that go to form its mental pole. Out of its own internal relations to a world which is itself capable of external relations, it acquires its own extensive region, which constitutes it as a discrete entity. This is what enables Whitehead to say "It is by means of 'extension' that the bonds between prehensions take on the dual aspect of internal relations which are yet in a sense external relations" (PR, 471).

Other comments on the problem of internal relations will be made at appropriate points. It should be mentioned that many discussions of the internal relations problem—Ewing's, for example—do not shed much light on Whitehead's theory of the internal relations among actual entities. Such discussions are perhaps more suited to a context where the terms are static, as in logic. This also applies to certain of Whitehead's discussions of 'settled' relations—i.e. relations between completed actual entities in a 'nexus.' This type of relation is more analogous to his discussion of the relations among eternal objects than to his discussion of the relations in a concrescence. There is a difference, that is to say, between a relation in the sense of a feeling by a new actual entity of some past settled actual entities, and a relation in the sense of the various bonds among the settled entities that make them, as felt, a unity. When A feels B, there is a certain kind of togetherness; when A feels B and C, part of the togetherness of B and C is given by the fact that they are both felt by A. If B and C are both felt by A, they form part of what is called a 'contrast,' and in one sense of relation, a relation is a genus of contrasts.[2]

We may now return to our discussion of the physical pole. The physical pole of an actual entity can be thought of as the sum of the internal relations that entity has to other actual entities.

> All entities, including even other actual entities, enter into the self-realization of an actuality in the capacity of determinants of the definiteness of that actuality (PR, 340).

2. See section CIII of this chapter.

In these terms, an actual entity is a real togetherness of other actual entities, and because the definiteness of any actual entity is given by forms, or eternal objects, an actual entity is thought of as a real togetherness [3] of eternal objects. This togetherness is elsewhere qualified as an 'experiential togetherness,' which is a "togetherness of its own kind, explicable by reference to nothing else." [4] The following passage states the ultimate character of this togetherness and thus amplifies the Category of the Ultimate.

> The novel entity is at once the togetherness of the 'many' which it finds, and also it is one among the disjunctive 'many' which it leaves; it is a novel entity, disjunctively among the many entities which it synthesizes. . . .
>
> Thus the 'production of novel togetherness' is the ultimate notion embodied in the term 'concrescence.' These ultimate notions of 'production of novelty' and of 'concrete togetherness' are inexplicable either in terms of higher universals or in terms of the components participating in the concrescence (PR, 32).

However inexplicable this togetherness may be, in talking about it it is necessary at least to characterize it; and Whitehead does so, calling it 'togetherness in a feeling.' Here one touches on the heart of Whitehead's ontology, for it appears that a feeling is in turn nothing but one of the peculiar characteristics of the togetherness: there is no feeler over and above the togetherness which is the feeling. The physical pole is the sum of the internal relations of a given actual entity to other actual entities; these relations are the determinate ways in which the other entities are felt, and they are spoken of as *internal* because the entity is merely the togetherness of these feelings. It

3. According to Whitehead, the 'real constitution' of an actual entity is given by the eternal objects functioning "by introducing the multiplicity of actual entities as constitutive of the actual entity in question. Thus the constitution is 'real' because it assigns its status in the real world to the actual entity" (PR, 93). Somewhat later, the same notion is spoken of as the 'real essence,' "the 'organic doctrine' demands a 'real essence' in the sense of a complete analysis of the relations, and inter-relations of the actual entities which are formative

only remains to notice that the togetherness of the feelings is after all only a certain kind of novel togetherness of
the actual entities forming the universe at a given point.

II.

THE CONTRAST DEVELOPED: THE DOCTRINE OF PREHENSIONS; THE ROLE OF ETERNAL OBJECTS

The more general term for the components of an actual entity is 'prehension.' Prehensions include feelings of
other actual entities, feelings of eternal objects, and exclusions of the latter from feeling, these exclusions being
spoken of as 'negative prehensions.' 'Feeling,' then, is
identical with 'positive prehension'; and there are also
negative prehensions, which exclude from feeling.

> The philosophy of organism is a cell-theory of actuality.
> Each ultimate unit of fact is a cell-complex, not analysable
> into components with equivalent completeness of actu-
> ality. . . .
> In the genetic-theory, the cell is exhibited as appro-
> priating, for the foundations of its own existence, the
> various elements of the universe out of which it arises.
> Each process of appropriation of a particular element is
> termed a prehension. The ultimate elements of the uni-
> verse, thus appropriated, are the already constituted ac-
> tual entities, and the eternal objects. All the actual entities
> are positively prehended but only a selection of the eter-
> nal objects (PR, 334–35).

> An actual entity in the actual world of a subject *must* enter
> into the concrescence of that subject by some simple
> casual feeling, however vague, trivial and submerged. . . .
> In the case of an eternal object there is no such necessity.
> . . . The actualities *have* to be felt, while the pure poten-
> tials *can* be dismissed (PR, 366).

of the actual entity in question, and an 'abstract essence' in which
the specified actual entities are replaced by the notions of unspecified
entities in *such* a combination; this is the notion of an unspecified
actual entity" (*loc. cit.*). For another remark on the part eternal
objects play, see PR, 147.
4. PR, 288; cf. PR, 48, "All real togetherness is togetherness in the
formal constitution of an actuality."

With these few preliminaries, it is now possible to contrast the physical pole with the mental pole.

> In each concrescence there is a twofold aspect of the creative urge. In one aspect there is the origination of simple causal feelings; and in the other aspect there is the origination of conceptual feelings. These contrasted aspects will be called the physical and the mental poles of an actual entity. No actual entity is devoid of either pole; though their relative importance differs in different actual entities (PR, 366).

What is here called a 'causal feeling' is more often called a 'physical feeling' which, as a 'feeling of another actuality,' [5] has just been described. Physical feelings may be effectively compared with conceptual feelings by saying that the other actual entities given to an actual entity must in some way be felt by it, and in such a way as to render the feeler, in respect of these feelings, complete, determinate, and settled. But the actual world, i.e. the totality of the felt actual entities, does not determine just how it is to be felt: the internal relations an actual entity has with its actual world determine it, but it chooses in a measure the internal relations into which it will enter. The sense in which the actual world does not entirely determine how it is to be felt is the sense in which conceptual feeling is possible. On the other hand, it is possible for the actual world to be felt only because "the physical and other feelings originate as steps towards realizing . . . conceptual aim through their treatment of initial data" (PR, 342).

The notion of togetherness may now be broadened by saying that novel togetherness requires other elements than mere physical feelings, for in the latter case there could be no novelty: a physical feeling is the reiteration of an element of a concrete entity, and it is already a novelty

5. If an actual entity is at any given moment composed *entirely* of internal relations—that is, if its conceptual feelings are also, from its point of view, internal relations; and if these feelings, both physical and conceptual, tell the whole story of the entity; then the entity is completely determinate.

that only an element, and not the whole, is reiterated. In so far as physical feelings are dominant, an actual entity reproduces aspects of actual entities in its actual world; and in so far as conceptual feelings are present, there is novel togetherness.

At this point a short digression on the various types of feelings, or prehensions, is in order. In any prehension, to use the wider term, it is always some *entity* that is prehended, and the prehension in question is always a component of some *actual entity*. Basic prehensions will therefore be correlated with the basic entities prehended; and, these latter being of two types—actual entities and eternal objects—there will be two basic kinds of prehension: physical and conceptual. All more complicated prehensions are made up in some way of these basic types, together with 'transmuted feelings.'

> There are an indefinite number of types of feeling according to the complexity of the initial data which the feeling integrates, and according to the complexity of the objective datum which it finally feels. But there are three primary types of feeling which enter into the formation of all the more complex feelings. These types are: *i*] that of simple physical feelings, *ii*] that of conceptual feelings, and *iii*] that of transmuted feelings. In a simple physical feeling, the initial datum is a single actual entity, in a conceptual feeling, the objective datum is an eternal object, in a transmuted feeling, the objective datum is a nexus of actual entities. Simple physical feelings and transmuted feelings make up the class of physical feelings (PR, 354–55).

The status as entity of actual entities and eternal objects is clear enough. So is the status of a 'nexus,' for this is "a particular fact of togetherness among actual entities" (PR, 30), this togetherness being thought of as the relatedness constituted by the prehensions, one by another, of these actual entities.[6] But more complex prehensions or feelings

6. An excellent example of a nexus is the settled, completed universe of actual entities out of which a new actual entity grows. This is called the actual world of the new actual entity. This actual world has a unity derived partly from the fact that it is felt as a

are also feelings of entities: a 'propositional feeling,' for instance, is a feeling of a proposition, which is considered an entity. In order to maintain the position that a feeling is always the feeling of an entity, Whitehead is therefore forced to speak as though the integration of the feelings of basic entities produces not only a complex feeling, but also a new complex entity to be felt. Thus, in speaking of propositions, he says,

> Thus propositions grow with the creative advance of the world. They are neither pure potentials, nor pure actualities; they are a manner of potential nexus involving pure potentialities and pure actualities. They are a new type of entities. Entities of this impure type presuppose the two pure types of entities (PR, 287).

Apparently Whitehead wishes merely to stress the fact that whatever is a datum for a feeling has a unity as felt: if a certain set of basic entities is felt in a very complex way, then the feeling gives that complexity a unity. And this is apparently the meaning of the inclusion in the Categories of Existence of a number of types of entities over and above the basic ones. The seventeenth Category of Explanation expresses this thought, as well as the fact that the inclusion of 'contrasts' in the Categories of Existence makes provision for an indefinite number of entities.

> xvii] That whatever is a datum for feeling has a unity *as felt*. Thus the many components of a complex datum have a unity: this unity is a 'contrast' of entities. In a sense this means that there are an endless number of categories of

unity by the new actual entity, and partly from the fact that each of the members of the actual world in turn feels as a unity *its* actual world. Actual worlds form a hierarchy, "An actual world is a nexus; and the actual world of one actual entity sinks to the level of a subordinate nexus in actual worlds beyond that actual entity" (PR, 42). We have already met in passing the notion of 'contrasts'; a nexus is a contrast (PR, 349) in the sense that all the connectedness in it is ascribable to elements being held together in contrast in one feeling, or a hierarchy of such. Relations, in one sense of that word, are abstractable from contrasts. In another sense of relation, the feeling in which the contrasted elements are held is a relation.

existence, since the synthesis of entities into a contrast in general produces a new existential type. For example, a proposition is, in a sense, a 'contrast.' For the practical purposes of 'human understanding' it is sufficient to consider a few basic types of existence, and to lump the more derivative types together under the heading of 'contrasts' . . . (PR, 36).

The unity of a datum, then, comes either solely from the two basic types of entities, or from these plus the unity of the subject's feeling; in the latter case the feeling is complex, and is said to be of a complex entity.

After this exposition, it may be profitable to present the more basic feelings in tabular form. In the following table the only entities involved are actual entities, eternal objects, and nexus. If the table were to include more complex entities, it could only do so by displaying these as more complex feelings.

Some account of the place eternal objects have in physical feelings is also needed. All conceptual feelings are of eternal objects, but it seems that even physical feelings as such involve eternal objects. An eternal object is a 'form of definiteness' (PR, 32), or a 'potentiality' of definiteness for any actual existence (PR, 63); so that any actual entity, considered as determinate and settled, and entering as felt into some other actual entity, i.e. as 'objectified,' has its definiteness entirely by way of eternal objects. For this reason, when the definiteness of an actual entity is felt, it is the definiteness of the ingressing eternal objects that is felt. Whitehead's usage here is puzzling, but I think without ambiguity. In general he uses the term 'conceptual feeling' only when speaking of the mental pole; when he wishes to refer to an eternal object in its role as the mediator in the definiteness involved in a physical feeling, he speaks of its 'dative ingression,' and its 'two-way functioning.' These two terms are not exactly synonymous. 'Dative ingression' refers to the functioning of an eternal object by means of which it presents for objectification some element in the definiteness of an actual entity that is in the actual world of some new actual

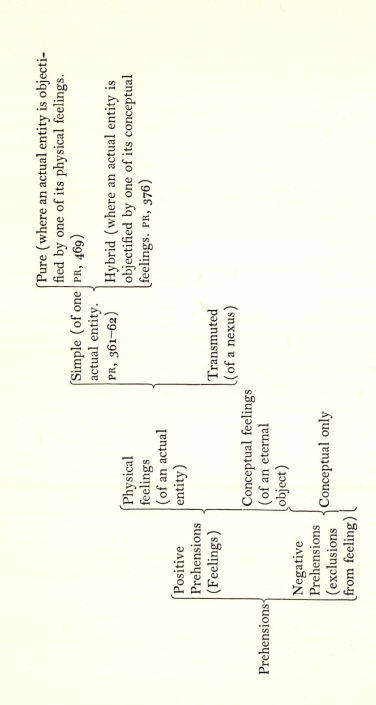

Prehensions

Positive Prehensions (Feelings)

Physical feelings (of an actual entity)

Simple (of one actual entity. PR, 361–62)

Pure (where an actual entity is objectified by one of its physical feelings. PR, 469)

Hybrid (where an actual entity is objectified by one of its conceptual feelings. PR, 376)

Transmuted (of a nexus)

Conceptual feelings (of an eternal object)

Negative Prehensions (exclusions from feeling)

Conceptual only

entity, this element being still indeterminate as to how—if at all—it is to be included, i.e. objectified, in the new actual entity. Thus,

> An eternal object when it has ingression through its function of objectifying the actual world, so as to present the datum for prehension, is functioning 'datively.' Hence, to sum up, there are four modes of functioning whereby an eternal object has ingression into the constitution of an actual entity: *i*] as dative ingression, *ii*] in conformal feeling, *iii*] in conceptual feeling, *iv*] in comparative feeling (PR, 249).

'Two-way functioning,' on the other hand, is the function-ing of an eternal object not in *presenting* an element for objectification, but in *objectifying* it, and that in such a way that the element is reproduced in the feeler. It would thus fall under (*ii*) in the above quotation. It is discussed as follows.

> A simple physical feeling enjoys a characteristic which has been variously described as 're-enaction,' 'reproduc-tion,' and 'conformation.' This characteristic can be more accurately explained in terms of the eternal objects in-volved. There are eternal objects determinant of the def-initeness of the objective datum which is the 'cause,' and eternal objects determinant of the subjective form belong-ing to the 'effect.' When there is re-enaction there is one eternal object with two-way functioning, namely, as partial determinant of the objective datum, and as partial deter-minant of the subjective form (PR, 364).

Whitehead does indeed sometimes seem to speak of an eternal object in its two-way functioning as conceptually felt. Thus in the following two Categoreal Obligations, it would seem that the notion 'conceptual feeling' is applied first to the physical pole (Category *iv*), and then to the mental pole (Category *v*).

> *iv*] *The Category of Conceptual Valuation.*
> From each physical feeling there is the derivation of a purely conceptual feeling whose datum is the eternal object determinant of the definiteness of the actual entity, or of the nexus, physically felt.

v] *The Category of Conceptual Reversion.*
There is secondary origination of conceptual feelings with data which are partially identical with, and partially diverse from, the eternal objects forming the data in the first phase of the mental pole. The diversity is a relevant diversity determined by the subjective aim.

Note that Category (*iv*) concerns conceptual reproduction of physical feeling, and Category (*v*) concerns conceptual diversity from physical feeling (PR, 39–40).

But Category (*iv*) does not really concern physical feelings, because there is a difference between a physical feeling (which is itself a reproduction) and a *"conceptual* reproduction of physical feeling" (which is a reproduction of a reproduction: a *mental*, though unconscious, reproduction of the kind of reproduction that belongs to the physical pole). To take the contrast to a different context from that of Whitehead's, there is a difference between a man's inheriting brown hair from his father, and a man's being aware that some other man has brown hair.

But when the definiteness of another actual entity is physically felt, although Whitehead does not use the term 'conceptual feeling' to describe what takes place, what is felt is nevertheless the definiteness of the eternal objects having ingression into the felt actual entity.[7] And this seems to come very close to dissolving physical feelings into the feelings of eternal objects. Perhaps this is ultimately the case in Whitehead's philosophy, but it is nevertheless true that an actual entity that is physically felt does not contribute *merely* definiteness, as we learn from the twentieth Category of Explanation.

xx] That to 'function' means to contribute determination to the actual entities in the nexus of some actual world. . . . 'Determination' is analysable into 'definiteness' and 'position,' where 'definiteness' is the illustration of select eternal objects, and 'position' is relative status in a nexus of actual entities (PR, 38).

Thus the peculiarly physical thing about a physical feeling is its vectoral character. A physical thing, or *real*

7. For a sketch of this functioning of eternal objects, see PR, 445.

togetherness of eternal objects, is the *datum,* and the eternal objects having ingression into the actual entity in question are not themselves *data,* but function datively in respect of the actual entity in which they have ingression. The vectoral character of physical feelings depends upon the "positions" of the felt entities, and it would seem that over and above the eternal objects that give an actual entity its definiteness, only these "positions" remain.

We have, however, already met with eternal objects of the objective species, and we have noticed the part they play in extensiveness; [8] and an attempt will be made later [9] to show that even the "position" of an actual entity consists of a certain togetherness of eternal objects. Should this prove convincing, it will seem that the togetherness of eternal objects gives an actual entity its whole character, except the character of the togetherness that justifies our referring to it as togetherness in a *feeling.* The exception may be illusory. The question will later be raised whether the notion 'togetherness in a feeling' conveys anything more than 'togetherness' when there is no subject for the feeling (except as a togetherness of feelings), and when the whole subjective character of the feeling is given in terms of eternal objects.[10]

III.

THE UNITY OF THE ACTUAL ENTITY

Such abstractions as 'physical pole,' 'mental pole,' 'physical feeling,' and 'conceptual feeling' falsely suggest a composite character that an actual entity does not have: one is tempted to think of a physical feeling to which a conceptual feeling is added as a kind of novel reaction. This difficulty probably arises through the fact that there is a successiveness to the physical pole, since an actual entity has a development, which suggests a corresponding successiveness in the mental pole. A passage like the fol-

8. See section A1 of this chapter.
9. See section D of this chapter.
10. See the discussion of 'subjective form' in section D of this chapter.

lowing insists upon the unity of the actual entity, the while it detracts from that unity by way of the succession it suggests in the mental pole.

> This doctrine of the inherence of the subject in the process of its production requires that in the primary phase of the subjective process there be a conceptual feeling of subjective aim: the physical and other feelings originate as steps toward realizing this conceptual aim through their treatment of initial data. This basic conceptual feeling suffers simplification in the successive phases of the concrescence. It starts with conditioned alternatives, and by successive decisions is reduced to coherence (PR, 342).

The difficulty is lessened if such a passage is read with the thought in mind that the unity of an actual entity is derived from its mental pole. This tentative solution brings problems for freedom, which are discussed at some length in chapters 3 and 4. But here the concern is with the light it might shed on the relation of the physical and the mental pole. Let us therefore consider in a preliminary way the difficulty and the tentative solution.

All succession belongs to the physical pole, but the determinate physical feelings that make up the physical pole are abstracted from the actual world by the selective action of the mental pole: the mental pole does not only add novel emphasis, it also selects the physical feelings that are to be incorporated. But this succession in the physical pole seems to infect the mental pole when we try to isolate the latter—because we can only know the latter by its results. Consider such a passage as the following.

> The mental pole is the subject determining its own ideal of itself by reference to eternal principles of valuation autonomously modified in their application to its own physical objective datum. Every actual entity is 'in time' so far as its physical pole is concerned, and is 'out of time' so far as its mental pole is concerned. It is the union of two worlds, namely, the temporal world, and the world of autonomous valuation. The integration of each simple physical feeling with its conceptual counterpart produces in a subsequent phase a physical feeling whose subjective

form of re-enaction has gained or lost subjective intensity according to the valuation up, or the valuation down, in the conceptual feeling (PR, 380).

Here, if one talks of a 'subsequent phase' he can only mean a phase revealed by the physical pole. Yet what is one to make of the many passages in which Whitehead seems to speak of the phases of the mental pole?

> This basic conceptual feeling [conceptual feeling of subjective aim] suffers simplification in the successive phases of the concrescence (PR, 342).

> Each temporal unity, in one sense, originates from its mental pole, analogously to God himself. It derives from God its basic conceptual aim, relevant to its actual world, yet with indeterminations, awaiting its own decisions. This subjective aim in its successive modifications remains the unifying factor governing the successive phases of interplay between physical and conceptual feelings (PR, 343).

Such passages are numerous.[11] Their general tenor is, on the one hand, to insist upon the indivisibility of the mental pole, and upon the fact that it is out of time; and, on the other, to talk of 'phases' when speaking of such ingredients of the mental pole as subjective aim. One can piece out a tentative interpretation if one remembers that "The integration of the physical and mental side into the unity of experience is a self-formation which is a process of concrescence" (PR, 165). Since the subjective aim is just what controls this integration, it is in one sense the mental pole regarded as controlling, unifying, and adding to the physical feelings. In another sense it is the physical pole regarded as subject to this integration, since the aim is, having regard to the development of the entity as a whole, always *from* a given integration of physical with conceptual feelings. Much of chapters 3 and 4 will be taken up with this problem, and the interpretation there set forth will also bear upon the difficulties noticed in chapter 1 about the identification of self-causation (self-creation),

11. See for instance PR, 227–28.

subjective aim, and final causation. It need only be noticed at present that if the mental pole is regarded as
unalterable, then self-causation must be identified either
with (*a*) the achievement of the full subjective aim (including the elements of the initial subjective aim given by
God, but other elements as well) by the entity "all at
once," the subjective aim then proceeding to control the
integration of mental and physical feelings, or with (*b*)
the *integration* of the mental and physical pole.

B.

'Subjective aim' | 'objectification'

The discussion in the previous section has already
anticipated some of the characteristics of subjective aim,
and the conception of an entity as the *integration* of a
mental pole and a physical pole has suggested a possible
explanation for some of the ambiguity of Whitehead's
utterances on subjective aim. Yet it is clear that, if the
notion of subjective aim does suffer an ambiguity because
of the fact that the aim is always *from* a physical pole (or
from a given integration of physical feelings with conceptual prehensions) and *towards* a mental pole, or totality of
the conceptual feelings controlling a given integration, it
is the latter with which subjective aim is in the main
specifically identified.

As such it stands, taken as a component of a given
entity, in contrast with a set of objectifications forming
other components of the same entity. *a)* It is, in the first
place, that which has guided the objectifications up to any
given point in the actual entity's history, both as to the
selection of the elements to be objectified from the actual
world existing at the start of a new actual entity, and as to
the *way* in which these objectifications are to be integrated in (felt by) the new actual entity. *b)* It is also
that which in the later course of the entity's development
will select still further elements of the actual world to be
objectified and will determine just how they are to be felt.
The actual world is what is given to an actual entity at its

inception; the objectified world is a selection of elements from each of the members of the actual world, the selection being felt physically, and contributing thereby to the determinateness of the actual entity. By this account, subjective aim selects conditions (objectifications) from a wider sphere of conditions (actual world), and incorporates the chosen conditions in a togetherness that is a novelty as over against both spheres.

The distinction between the terms 'actual world' and 'objectification' can be made more precise. The meaning of 'actual world' is given as follows.

> The nexus of actual entities in the universe correlate to a concrescence, is termed 'the actual world' correlate to that concrescence (PR, 34).

Each actual entity in the actual world must be physically felt by the actual entity to whom that actual world is given, but "each entity in the universe of a given concrescence *can*, so far as its own nature is concerned, be implicated in that concrescence in one or another of many modes; but *in fact* it is implicated only in one mode" (PR, 34). The way in which the actual world is in fact implicated constitutes the objectified world of a given actual entity.

> The term 'objectification' refers to the particular mode in which the potentiality of one actual entity is realized in another actual entity (PR, 34).

In speaking of 'simple physical feelings'—which represent the simplest instance of objectification, since only one actual entity is then felt—Whitehead distinguishes between the actual entity as *initial* datum of the feeling and as *objective* datum of the feeling (PR, 361). In the latter case not the entity as a whole but rather one of *its* feelings is felt: the entity is objectified by one of its feelings. This distinction between 'initial datum' and 'objective datum' is the distinction between the actual world and a set of objectifications reduced to its lowest terms.

It should not be forgotten that the actual world be-

comes the objectified world by virtue of the initial subjective aim, supplied by God as 'principle of concretion,' in
which capacity he brings an entity out of an *impasse*
riddled with ambiguity. Our discussion therefore embraces both the doctrine that physical feelings are only
possible by means of the mental pole and the doctrine
that an actual entity consists in the concrescence of physical and mental feelings. The actual world and the objectified world express the factor of condition in different
degrees of proximity to a new actual entity. The question
of the distinction between 'subjective aim' and 'initial
subjective aim' will be deferred until chapter 3.

C.

'Novelty', 'creative advance', 'intensity' | 'conformation', 'reproduction'

i.

'GENETIC DIVISION' AND 'COORDINATE DIVISION'; THE 'EPOCHAL' THEORY OF TIME

This contrast will be more intelligible if it is introduced by some discussion of the 'phases' of feeling. The
various *types* of feeling have already been discussed; we
shall now be concerned with their *integration* in the genesis of an actual entity.

Our account focuses upon the *concrescence* of an actual entity rather than upon its status as *concrete* and
complete, but as this distinction is partly given in terms of
a distinction between the 'genetic division' and the 'coordinate division' of an actual entity we shall begin with an
account of the latter distinction. We shall then turn to the
'epochal' theory of time, which is also a necessary preliminary for a consideration of the phases of feeling.

Division of the entity in concrescence is called 'genetic
division'; division of the completed, or 'satisfied,' entity is
called 'coordinate division' (PR, 433–36). If we attend to
the character of an entity in process and to the full immediacy of its feeling, we speak of its genetic division or of
its *formal* existence; if we think of the entity as complete,
and as such felt by some future entity, we speak of its

coordinate division, of its 'satisfaction,' or of its existence *objectivé*. The distinction is of course Descartes'; the term *'objectivé,'* as developed by Descartes in the Third Meditation, brings with it, however, the doctrine of representative ideas, so that it is best to take the terms in just the sense Whitehead specifies. In its coordinate division a felt actual entity forms, together with all the other actual entities in the actual world of some new actual entity, a space-time continuum, or 'extensive continuum.' In thus forming part of a continuum, the space-time region proper to any actual entity is divisible, "although in the genetic growth it is undivided" (PR, 435).

The undivided character of the genetic growth is the sense in which the extensive continuum is the result of the atomic development of extensiveness, as we shall see in the following discussion of the epochal theory of time. But the coordinate division of the actual entities in the actual world of some new entity does not yield only the extensive continuum—this is rather the most general fact derived from such division—it yields also a set of finished, completed feelings, or prehensions, which in turn can be felt by a new actual entity. This is the 'public' side of any complex datum.

> An actual entity considered in reference to the publicity of things is a 'superject'; namely, it arises from the publicity which it finds, and it adds itself to the publicity which it transmits. It is a moment of passage from decided public facts to a novel public fact. *Public facts are in their nature, coordinate* (PR, 443; italics supplied).

This is summarized by saying that "Prehensions have public careers, but they are born privately" (PR, 444). It should be noted that when a feeling of a completed actual entity is felt much of the subjectivity is lost.

> the coordinate division of an actual entity produces feelings whose subjective forms are partially eliminated and partially inexplicable (PR, 447).[12]

12. The matters here sketched are discussed in part in PR, part IV, chapter I; there is a brief summary on the concluding page of the chapter, p. 448.

A full understanding of genetic division is of course dependent upon an account of the epochal theory of time. By the epochal[13] theory, neither the mental nor the physical pole of an actual entity can be said to be in time. But though both poles are out of time, genetic phases are discernible in the concrescence of the entity and these lend to time some of its features. The fact of genetic divisibility is what Whitehead means when he says that "the creature is extensive"; that "in every act of becoming there is the becoming of something with temporal extension" (PR, 107); that there is a "becoming of continuity"; or that "extensiveness becomes" (PR, 53). On the other hand he insists that both poles of an entity are out of time (or undivided) when he opposes to these notions the ideas that the "act of becoming [of the creature] is not extensive" (PR, 107); that there is "no continuity of becoming," or that "becoming itself is not extensive" (PR, 53); that "in the genetic growth [the region] is undivided" (PR, 435); or that the "genetic process presupposes the entire quantum" (PR, 434) of space and time.

What is important now is that in its concrescence an entity is divisible, and that phases are therefore discernible within it. The problem at once arises that the mental pole is not only out of time but is also indivisible. This applies both to genetic division,[14] which we are now discussing, and to coordinate division as well. From a passage concerned with the latter, we can take a claim that holds for both kinds of division: "The concrescence is dominated by a subjective aim which essentially concerns the creature as a final superject" (PR, 108). Elsewhere, in less guarded speech than that we have seen him use in connection with the epochal theory of time, Whitehead says that "Every actual entity is 'in time' so far as its physical pole is concerned, and is 'out of time' so far as its mental pole is concerned" (PR, 380). There is good reason for the expression "less guarded," for on the epochal

13. See SMW, chapter VII, especially pp. 175–80; PR, 105–8, 188–95, 222, 434, 486–90.
14. PR, 380; cf. chapter 3, p. 105.

theory the "genetic passage from phase to phase is not in physical time: the exactly converse point of view expresses the relationships of concrescence to physical time. . . . Physical time expresses some features of the growth, but *not* the growth of the features. . . . The actual entity is the enjoyment of a certain quantum of physical time" (PR, 434).

But at least it is clear that the mental pole is indivisible, and the physical pole has a divisibility that lends to extensiveness some of its features. And of course the epochal character of time—the character by which it appears in the form of atomic 'arrests,' or 'durations'—depends upon the indivisibility of the mental pole; for this indivisibility commands that the divisibility of the physical pole shall mean merely that the entity as a whole 'enjoys' a quantum of time. To say that the extensive side of an actual entity is its physical pole is merely to repeat the earlier assertions that "extensiveness becomes," or "there is a becoming of continuity." The correlate of these assertions was that the act of becoming is not extensive; and this means merely that "the genetic process [which includes the physical pole] presupposes the entire quantum of space and time."

The features of the epochal theory of time that are important for the discussion of an actual entity as a concrescence of feelings may now be summarized. *a)* Time is given in quanta, or durations. *b)* The actual entity, in taking a full perspective of the totality of other actual entities, is what makes these quanta, or durations, (as well as what enjoys them) and therefore is not "in" time. *c)* The actual entity is divisible in respect of its physical pole, and this divisibility is what gives time some of its features—this being expressed by saying that there is a "becoming of continuity" and that "extensiveness becomes." *d)* The physical pole is out of time, in a less complete way than is the mental pole, because the physical pole lends to time some of its features, and because it is dependent for its unity on the mental pole. The exemption of the physical pole from being "in" time is expressed

in the notions that "there is no continuity of becoming"
and "the act of becoming [of the creature] is not extensive." *e*) Physical time and space appear in the coordinate division of an actual entity: the extensive continuum
is the result of the togetherness of completed actual entities, the divisibility of whose physical poles reflects the
character of the genetic growth into the coordinate division. Time is atomic, in that it grows by arrests or durations that are not in time; time is a continuum, in that it is
the togetherness of such durations taken in their divisibility. Its atomic character belongs to the genesis, its character as continuum to the coordinate division.

II.

THE PHASES OF FEELING: INTRODUCTION

These considerations are necessary before the phases
of an entity can be discussed, and these phases are required for the understanding of the contrast that is at
present under discussion. What should have emerged
from the remarks on the epochal character of time is the
awareness that when one speaks of the various 'phases' in
which conceptual and physical feelings are integrated, the
question of the reality of these 'phases,' except in regard to
the divisibility of the physical pole, must be raised. When
one says that in such and such a phase conceptual feelings
arise, one may be looking at the conceptual feelings, so to
speak, from the side of the physical pole. Now a subjective
aim is a kind of conceptual feeling, and the reality of the
development of subjective aim, and therefore of the reality of self-causation, may be called in question. The matter is here raised as a problem; it will be dealt with more
extensively in chapter 3.

With this qualification, the phases of concrescence
may now be introduced.

> The process of concrescence is divisible into an initial
> stage of many feelings, and a succession of subsequent
> phases of more complex feelings integrating the earlier
> simpler feelings, up to the satisfaction which is one com-
> plex unity of feeling. This is the 'genetic' analysis of the

satisfaction. . . . A feeling—i.e. a positive prehension—is essentially a transition effecting a concrescence. Its complex constitution is analysable into five factors which express what that transition consists of, and effects. The factors are: *i*] the 'subject' which feels, *ii*] the 'initial data' which are to be felt, *iii*] the 'elimination' in virtue of negative prehensions, *iv*] the 'objective datum' which is felt, *v*] the 'subjective form' which is *how* that subject feels that objective datum (PR, 337–38).

The phases are first divided into two broad phases: *a)* the 'receptive,' 'responsive,' or 'conformal' phase, or 'phase of enjoyment,' in which a *vector* character is dominant, and *b)* the 'supplemental phase,' or phase of 'emotion' or 'appetition,' in which a *scalar* character is predominant. The phases are terminated by the 'satisfaction,' which is "merely the culmination marking the evaporation of all indetermination; so that in respect to all modes of feeling and to all entities in the universe, the satisfied actual entity embodies a determinate attitude of 'yes' or 'no.' "[15] (PR, 323). The relevance to the fundamental contrast now under discussion may be indicated by saying that 'conformation' and 'reproduction' belong to the first phase; while 'creative advance,' 'novelty,' 'subjective intensity' belong to the supplemental phase. Some environments exact more conformation than others,[16] and so the supplemental phase may afford more or less novelty; but it is important that a supplemental phase is always present in some form.

The nature of the first phase—the receptive, conformal, reproductive, or responsive—can perhaps best be seen in simple actual entities in which there is "negligible autonomous energy" (PR, 374), and in which, therefore,

15. In our discussion of phases, the terminology is perhaps more systematic and consistent than in Whitehead's own usage. 'Supplemental' seems occasionally, e.g., PR, 273, to be applied to one of the *sub*-phases of what is here called 'supplemental'; this may be because in less highly developed actual entities only the first element of the supplemental phase is present.
16. This point will be considered towards the end of the chapter; it suggests that the factor of condition may be thought of not only as imposing limitations but also as affording opportunity.

the supplemental phase, though necessarily present, is also negligible in its complexity and in the novelty introduced. If we wish to look at the conformal phase as the only important phase in an actual entity, we can say that "The conformal stage merely transforms the objective content into subjective feelings" (PR, 250), and add that this tells the whole story of the entity in question. If we wish to cover this case and more complicated cases as well we can say that "The responsive [i.e. conformal] phase absorbs . . . data as material for a subjective unity of feeling" (PR, 261). In the present case we shall simply assume that the actual entity in question is negligible in the content of its supplemental phases.

There are three factors that are of particular importance in conformal feelings: the vector character, or reference to the datum; the role played by eternal objects; and the quantitative character, or the intensity, of the emotion involved. A] The notion of a vector reference forbids that the feeling be thought of as static, and insures a connection of the theory with the usual interpretation of the facts of physics; it also means that the definiteness of the feeling does not constitute the whole of the feeling, there being always a reference of the definiteness to this source. It has already been remarked that even the vectoral character of a feeling seems to depend upon eternal objects (of the objective species), and this problem will be raised again.

B] Eternal objects are said to supply the definiteness of the feeling; they therefore carry in the present context the main burden of the notion of reproduction or conformation, for the eternal object in the case of conformal feelings has a two-way functioning.

> A simple physical feeling enjoys a characteristic which has been variously described as 're-enaction,' 'reproduction,' and 'conformation.' This characteristic can be more accurately explained in terms of the eternal objects involved. There are eternal objects determinant of the definiteness of the objective datum which is the 'cause,' and

eternal objects determinant of the definiteness of the subjective form belonging to the 'effect.' When there is re-
enaction there is one eternal object with two-way functioning, namely, as partial determinant of the objective datum,
and as partial determinant of the subjective form. In this
two-way rôle, the eternal object is functioning relationally
between the initial data on the one hand and the concrescent subject on the other. It is playing one self-consistent
rôle in obedience to the category of objective identity (PR,
364).

The vector character together with this two-way functioning of the eternal objects insures that this will be a transfer of feeling—a feeling out *there* is *re-enacted here;* but
as Whitehead says, the re-enaction is no mere representa-
tion, but rather the real flow of the universe, upon which
the irreversibility of time depends.

> But this transference of feeling effects a partial identifica-
> tion of cause with effect, and not a mere representation of
> the cause. It is the cumulation of the universe and not a
> stage-play about it (PR, 363).

This is also expressed by saying that the cause is in the
effect objectively, "in virtue of being the feeler of the
feeling reproduced in the effect with partial equivalence
of subjective form" (PR, 363).

c] Any entity, thought of as an act of feeling, has a
subjective intensity, whose degree is measured by the
importance of the supplemental phase. In an entity where
only the conformal phase is nontrivial, the intensity of the
new entity varies little from that of the old. The question
of intensity is of course not really separable from the
matter of the two-way functioning of eternal objects. The
main point at issue is that the subjective form is repeated
with but slight variation, and that the subjective form has
a qualitative and a quantitative side, which are not separable. Eternal objects in their two-way functioning express the *qualitative* repetition; and since intensity is the
measure of the number of qualitative components held in

a contrast without incompatibility, there will also be a repetition of intensity. The repetition will not be exact because the new actual entity has its own mental pole: it will therefore have its own supplemental phase, however negligible. There will therefore be some difference in the new qualitative pattern, and the new subjective intensity will depend on this, being, as the case may be, negligibly more, negligibly less, or just the same; and in any case it will be negligible as over against the conformal side. This problem is taken up again in section D of this chapter, in connection with the discussion of subjective form.

III.

THE NATURE OF CONTRASTS

We now digress to develop Whitehead's notion of 'contrast.' As always, his formal definition is not to be overlooked: contrasts are "Modes of Synthesis of Entities in one Prehension" (PR, 33). Elsewhere a contrast is described as the unity a complex datum has *as felt* (PR, 36). Notice that togetherness in a feeling, or prehension, which is the basic fact in the emergence of the one out of the many, is stressed here; and as it is one of Whitehead's ultimate notions, there is perhaps no need to go behind it. The *many* of the world are together in this *one* feeling. But the conditions of that togetherness must be examined. The fundamental requirements are *a)* that "a complex unity must provide for each of its components a real diversity of status, with a reality which bears the same sense as its own reality and is peculiar to itself" (PR, 348); and *b)* that the diverse elements be combined in a real unity (PR, 344). The requirements are summarized in the following passage.

This diversity of status, combined with the real unity of the components, means that the real synthesis of two component elements in the objective datum of a feeling must be infected with the individual particularities of each of its relata. . . . A complex entity with this individual definiteness, arising out of determinateness of eternal objects, will be termed a 'contrast' (PR, 348-49).

But not merely *any* two elements or group of elements can enter into a contrast. 'Contrast' is the opposite of incompatibility and "depends on a certain simplicity of circumstance" (PR, 145). This simplicity of circumstance is associated with the notion of an 'order' in the universe. It is best exemplified in the simplicity of mathematical ratios, and best appears, in less abstract circumstances, in "the sharply distinguished genera and species which we find in nature" (PR, 145). I think it is fair to say that the notion of an order in the universe [17] is related to the activity of an actual entity by this notion of contrast: a contrast achieved in an entity or group of entities is, if transmitted, a kind of dominant order. In connection with the notion of layers of order, note the following, "Thus 'contrast'—as the opposite of incompatibility—depends on a certain simplicity of circumstance; but the higher contrasts depend on the assemblage of a multiplicity of lower contrasts, this assemblage again exhibiting higher types of simplicity" (PR, 145). I take it that one could regard the primordial nature of God as a contrast, and thus as that in the nature of things which determines whether certain elements are incompatible or capable of contrast. The source of order in the universe would therefore be the source of possible contrasts.

I have noticed that, in one sense of "relation," relations are abstracted from contrasts: "A relation can be found in many contrasts; and when it is so found, it is said to relate the things contrasted" (PR, 349). This is intended to overcome some of the difficulties (Whitehead cites Bradley) surrounding the relations problem, because a contrast is said to preserve both the discreteness of the terms, and the synthesis in virtue of which they are said to be (internally) related. But it is to be observed that this takes care of but one sense of relation (call it sense B), since the very prehension in which elements are held in contrast is itself a kind of relation (sense A). Evidently this latter kind of relation is a more ultimate notion, since it is produced by

17. See section E.

the growth of the universe; but the growth of the universe then results in new relations in the sense of abstraction from contrasts (sense B).

We here anticipate the discussion of the relations among eternal objects,[18] for a contrast is best understood in terms of eternal objects (PR, 349). Indeed, the contrast between any two actual entities seems always the contrast of the eternal objects that give each its definiteness. It would seem that a contrast differs from a mere disjunction in this sense, that the eternal objects in question (though their 'individual essences' are not affected) are, by the fact of contrast, required to enter into internal relations (as regards their 'relational essences') with one another. A contrast, then, really qualifies 'real potentiality.' The importance of this claim will not appear until chapters 5 and 6. But I would go on to observe that if contrasts *do* involve the qualification of the relational essences of eternal objects, then perhaps the togetherness in a contrast and, therefore, the togetherness in a feeling is really given by a certain kind of conjunction of internally related eternal objects. In this connection note the following remark on relations (sense B), "A 'relation' between occasions is an eternal object illustrated in the complex of mutual prehensions by virtue of which these occasions constitute a nexus" (PR, 295).

IV.

THE PHASES OF FEELING: CONCLUSION

After this discussion of the sense Whitehead gives his technical term 'contrast,' we return to the fundamental contrast (in our own nontechnical sense) that is the subject of sections Ci through Cv and take up again our discussion of conformal feelings.

Whitehead gives us a concrete instance of what he means by a conformal feeling when he states the theory in terms of the transmission of energy. Any actual entity is of course an example of the transmission of energy, whatever

18. See chapters 5 and 6.

else it may be. But if we consider an actual entity in whose concrescence only the conformal phase is of importance, we may think of the entity as merely an incident in energy transmission. Here "energy" is of course not equivalent with 'subjective intensity,' but is rather a special case of it: increase in subjective intensity brings with it no necessary increase in physical energy. But if we are speaking of an actual entity in which only the transmission of physical energy is of any importance, then we can say that the energy is a 'quantitative emotional intensity' which has a 'scalar localization'; that the form of the energy is given by the definiteness of what is felt, such definiteness being given by eternal objects of both the objective and subjective species; and that the vector-reference to the datum is "the basis of the vector-theory in physics" (PR, 177).

In the following passage on conformal feelings that are examples of energy transmission the 'sensa' correspond to the 'definiteness of what is felt' mentioned above, and they therefore consist of eternal objects of both species.[19] The definiteness of what is felt will be partly reproduced in the subjectivity of the new feeling, and partly passed along by the new entity as part of its objective definiteness. The definiteness of the felt entity therefore both contributes to the intensity of the energy (since its feelings, or subjective intensity, is reproduced) and determines the form the energy will take (since what is objective in it becomes objective in the new entity). The passage in question follows.

> Occasions A, B and C enter into the experience of occasion M as themselves experiencing sensa s_1 and s_2 unified by some faint contrast between s_1 and s_2. Occasion M responsively feels sensa s_1 and s_2 as its own sensations. There is thus a transmission of sensation emotion from A, B, and C to M. . . . Thus the (unconscious) direct perception of A, B, and C is merely the causal efficacy of A, B, and C as elements in the constitution of M . . . if A, B, and C tell the same tale with minor variations of intensity, the dis-

19. See PR, 446.

crimination of A, B, and C from each other will be irrelevant. There may thus remain a sense of the causal efficacy
of actual presences, whose exact relationships in the external world are shrouded. Thus the experience of M is to be
conceived as a quantitative emotion arising from the contribution of sensa from A, B, C and proportionately conformed to by M.

Generalizing from the language of physics, the experience of M is an intensity arising out of specific sensa,
directed from A, B, C. There is in fact a directed influx
from A, B, C of quantitative feeling, arising from specific
forms of feeling. The experience has a vector character, a
common measure of intensity, and specific forms of feeling
conveying that intensity. If we substitute the term 'energy'
for the concept of a quantitative emotional intensity, and
the term 'form of energy' for the concept of 'specific form
of feeling,' and remember that in physics 'vector' means
definite transmission from elsewhere, we see that this
metaphysical description of the simplest elements in the
constitution of actual entities agrees absolutely with the
general principles according to which the notions of modern physics are framed. The 'datum' in metaphysics is the
basis of the vector-theory in physics; . . . the 'sensa' in
metaphysics are the basis of the diversity of specific forms
under which energy clothes itself (PR, 176–77).

On the basis of what has already been said, sensa of the
objective species represent the form of the energy; while
sensa of the subjective species, in having to do with the
subjective intensity (in this case physical energy), furnish
an example of the two-way functioning of eternal objects,
which we have already met. The latter function of sensa
does not emerge from the foregoing passage, which is not
at best very clear. But what Whitehead has to say about
sensa in the context of his discussion of the two species of
eternal objects makes it clear not only that there is "intensity arising out of specific sensa," but also that some of
these sensa are *reproduced* in the subjective intensity of
the new actual entity.

The main point of this interpretation of transmission of
energy, taken as an example of conformal feelings, is that
the form of the energy is correlated with that which is

incurably *objective* in the satisfaction (or completed state) of an actual entity, while that which is a feeling in an old actual entity, and can be repeated in the feeling or *subjectivity* of a new actual entity, is correlated with the energy itself.

It is not possible here to attempt to find a way through the labyrinth of Whitehead's discussion of the passage from one phase of feeling to the next. The foregoing discussion of the conformal phase will serve as a sample of the very complex and detailed elaboration of the notion of feeling he provides. It is the main purpose of the present pages to complete the interpretation of the notion of phases that was begun earlier, with a view both to making it clear for its own sake and to elucidating by the way the contrast between conformation and reproduction on the one hand, and novelty, creative advance, and subjective intensity on the other. The interest will lie in how a "higher" phase represents a deviation from conformation, and an increase in subjective intensity, rather than in the various forms this deviation can take. I shall therefore merely sketch the various subphases of the supplemental phase, interpreting and simplifying Whitehead's account, before returning to examine the notion of successive phases.

The main course of the phases beyond conformal may be given by saying that the original physical feelings *give rise to* conceptual feelings. These conceptual feelings are then integrated with the physical feelings, to form new and more complex feelings. These complex feelings in turn may be integrated and reintegrated with the original feelings, until in a very complex phase of integration consciousness may arise.

All the phases beyond conformal are brought under the heading of the supplemental phase. The division of the supplemental phase in which physical feelings *give rise to* conceptual feelings is called   *a)* the 'aesthetic supplement,' or the phase of 'conceptual origination,' or of 'conceptual valuation.' [20] Here, in accordance with the

20. PR, 378 ff.

Categories of Conceptual Valuation, Conceptual Reversion,[21] and Transmutation,[22] there are, respectively, some
causal transference with detachment, some entrance of
novelty, and some abstraction from details. This is because, by conceptual reversion, not the prior entity is felt,
nor even one of that entity's conceptual feelings, but the
eternal objects that give that prior entity definiteness.[23] By
conceptual reproduction there is the integration with
these feelings of novel eternal objects (the first entrance
of absolute novelty); and by transmutation there is abstraction by which the common elements in a group of
actual entities are felt as characteristics of a nexus. When
the highest nontrivial phase of an actual entity is its
conformal phase, the entity is an example of the *transmission* of energy; when the aesthetic supplement is the highest nontrivial phase, the actual entity is an example of the
transformation of energy.[24]

When the aesthetic supplement is not the highest nontrivial phase in the concrescence of an actual entity, it
may be thought of as a valuation that is a necessary
preliminary to purpose. Purpose arises in *b)* the 'intellectual supplement,'[25] or phase of 'comparative feelings,'
where the valuations of phase (*a*) are integrated with the
physical feelings from which they originate to give the
phases of *1]* 'physical purposes,' *2]* 'propositional feelings,' and *3]* 'intellectual feelings,' in which, at last, consciousness arises.

21. PR, 39–40, 379–82.
22. PR, 40, 382–89.
23. This is a difficult conception, for *1)* a physical feeling of an
entity *a* by an entity *b*, *2)* a feeling of one of *a*'s conceptual
feelings by an entity *b*, and *3)* a conceptual feeling derived by *b*
from its physical feeling of *a*, are all of them bound up with the
definiteness *a* has by reason of the ingression into it of eternal
objects. The different feelings *b* may have are more readily understood by noting that in each case there is a causal influence of *a*
upon *b*, but with a growing detachment on the part of *b*, so that the
causal transference becomes less and less a reproduction of *a*. The
difficulty probably arises from the fact that the whole definiteness of
a is given in some fashion by eternal objects, *except* for the fact that
there is a vector from *a* to *b*, and from preceding actual entities to *a;*
this appears most clearly when one understands that a pure physical

A physical purpose arises "from the integration of a conceptual feeling with the basic feeling from which it is derived, either directly according to categoreal condition iv (the Category of Conceptual Valuation), or indirectly according to categoreal condition v (the Category of Conceptual Reversion). . . . The subjective forms of these physical purposes are either 'adversions' or 'aversions'" (PR, 406). What is felt is a contrast between the fact of the physical feeling and the valuation of abstract possibility embodied in the conceptual feeling; and the contrast is felt as compatible or as incompatible.[26] Evidently the Category of Transmutation is also involved, for in the following passage the physical feeling is spoken of as the feeling of a nexus; the passage also develops further the notions 'adversion,' and 'aversion.'

> In such a physical purpose, the datum is the generic contrast between the nexus, felt in the physical feeling, and the eternal object valued in the conceptual feeling. This eternal object is also exemplified as the pattern of the nexus. Thus the conceptual valuation now closes in upon the feeling of the nexus as it stands in the generic contrast, exemplifying the valued eternal object. This valuation according to the physical feeling endows the transcendent creativity with the character of adversion, or of aversion. The character of adversion secures the reproduction of the physical feeling, as one element in the objectification of the subject beyond itself. . . . It is felt and re-enacted down a route of occasions forming an enduring object.

feeling of an actual entity is the feeling of one of its actual feelings (whether conceptual or physical). But conceptual reproduction of a physical feeling of *a* by *b* means that *b* feels the eternal objects making up the definiteness of one of the physical feelings by *a* of some other actual entity, in abstraction from the vector character inherent in the physical feelings. The sense in which the vector character can be given by eternal objects of the objective species has been noticed.

24. PR, 389.

25. The term 'intellectual supplement' is a rather loose denomination, since this phase contains not only intellectual feelings, but also the feelings involved in physical purpose. The term 'comparative feelings' is more comprehensive.

26. PR, 421.

Finally this chain of transmission meets with incompatibilities, and is attenuated, or modified, or eliminated from further endurance.

When there is aversion, instead of adversion, the transcendent creativity assumes the character that it inhibits, or attenuates, the objectification of that subject in the guise of that feeling. . . . Thus adversions promote stability; and aversions promote change without any indication of the sort of change (PR, 422).

This quotation concerns primarily physical purpose in which the Category of Conceptual Valuation, but not the Category of Conceptual Reversion, plays a part. When reversion is also present with important intensity, there is "realization of the relevance of eternal objects as decided in the primordial nature of God," which are "effective feelings of the more remote alternative possibilities" (PR, 425). Reversion introduces new eternal objects, and therefore expresses the sense in which *contrast*, as a lure for intensity of feeling, is an exemplification of the Category of Subjective Intensity.[27] It will be remembered that "Each reverted conceptual feeling had its datum largely identical with that of its correlated primary feeling of the same pole" (PR, 425). In this instance the Category of Subjective Intensity is in point because "what is identical, and what is reverted, are determined by the aim at a favorable balance. The reversion is due to the aim at complexity as one condition of intensity" (PR, 425). Here "balance" means that "no realized eternal objects shall eliminate potential contrasts between other realized eternal objects"; and "complexity" means "realization of contrasts" (PR, 424).

The phase of physical purposes, considered generally,

27. PR, pp. 41, 424. This category offers certain difficulties. Self-causation can be understood as an aim at a "certain" subjective intensity. The present category speaks simply of an aim at intensity, and frequently in Whitehead's discussion of it one gets the impression that the category describes an aim at the highest possible intensity. It should be remembered, however, that the initial subjective aim is an aim at the best possible for a given situation, and if the full aim of an actual entity is not to be identical with initial

is the phase by which the transmission of feeling from one actual entity to the next gains a stability that makes 'enduring objects' possible; it is the phase in which there is "association of endurance with rhythm and physical valuation . . ." (PR, 426). Thus 'purpose' is here a technical term, not to be confused with conscious or unconscious purpose in living organisms.

Purpose in the more usual sense, when it is unconscious,[28] is made possible by the propositional feelings, which, in the intellectual supplement, or phase of comparative feelings, mediate between physical purposes and conscious intellectual feelings.

> The propositions are lures for feelings, and give to feelings a definiteness of enjoyment and purpose which is absent in the blank evaluation of physical feeling into physical purpose. In this blank evaluation we have merely the determination of the comparative creative efficacies of the component feelings of actual entities (PR, 427).

A proposition is defined in the fifteenth Category of Explanation.

> xv] That a proposition is the unity of certain actual entities in their potentiality for forming a nexus, with its potential relatedness partially defined by certain eternal objects which have the unity of one complex eternal object. The actual entities involved are termed the 'logical subject,' the complex eternal object is the 'predicate' (PR, 35–36).

We have here a) an abstraction from the actual entities, so that their definiteness is eliminated and they become mere relata; and b) a restriction of the absolute generality of the eternal objects in question, so that they are made to refer to just *these* actual entities.[29] But the propo-

subjective aim (a situation which would negate freedom) one must avoid thinking of the full subjective aim as necessarily an aim at the highest intensity. In this connection see chapter 3, pp. 123–24.

28. But note that consciousness also depends upon propositional feelings, "all forms of consciousness arise from ways of integration of propositional feelings with other feelings, either physical feelings or conceptual feelings" (PR, 391).

29. PR, 379.

sition always involves a merely *potential* qualification of the actual entities by the eternal objects; and the actual entities, though they are taken in some abstraction, must have those characteristics necessary for them to form a part of just *this* proposition.[30]

In so far as it is a potentiality a proposition resembles an eternal object. It is like an eternal object also in being a lure for feeling for *any* actual entity that has in its actual world the 'logical subjects' of the propositions, i.e. actual entities meeting the rather abstract requirements of the proposition. The requirement of partial limitation of the generality of the eternal objects forming the 'predicate,' and the requirement that the logical subjects possess certain characteristics, is expressed as follows.

> But particulars must be indicated; because the proposition concerns just those particulars and no others. Thus the indication belongs to the proposition; namely, 'Those particulars *as thus indicated* in such-and-such a predicative pattern' constitutes the proposition. Apart from the indication there is no proposition because there are no determinate particulars (PR, 295).

A propositional feeling can only arise after the phases that have already been discussed;[31] but it is of particular importance that, when felt, the proposition does not contribute to the definiteness of the actual entity that feels it in quite the same way as does an eternal object realized in physical purpose. In physical purpose "the eternal object as a mere potentiality, undetermined as to its physical realization, may lose its indetermination, i.e. its universality, by integration with itself as an element in the realized definiteness of the physical datum of the physical prehension. . . . the subjective form has acquired a special appetition—adversion or aversion—in respect to that eternal object as a realized element of definiteness in that physical datum" (PR, 280). But in a propositional feeling the proposition as felt always retains an indeterminateness, a

30. PR, 297.
31. PR, 397.

potentiality, which, while it gives "to feelings a definiteness of enjoyment and purpose which is absent in the
blank evaluation of physical feeling into physical purpose" (PR, 427), is always a feeling of a "sheer fact as a
possibility" (PR, 428).

Intellectual feelings arise from an integration of a propositional feeling with that feeling which 'indicates' the
actual entities that form the logical subject of the propositional feeling.

> In an intellectual feeling the datum is the generic con-
> trast between a nexus of actual entities and a proposition
> with its logical subjects members of the nexus (PR, 407).

They need no further description, as their importance
here lies in their forming the extreme of the long process
of integration and reintegration that I have summarized.
The phase of intellectual feelings is the phase in which
intensity of feeling, and therefore novelty, is at its height;
and it stands because of this at the opposite pole from the
conformal feelings, in which enhancement of intensity
and novelty is at a minimum. It now remains to reconsider
whether these 'phases' are properly so called.

Whitehead himself expresses some doubt on this point,
when, in talking of the two subphases of the supplemental
phase, he says ". . . the former—*so far as there is an
order*—is that of aesthetic supplement . . ." (Italics supplied, PR, 380).[32] But the clearest indication of the care
with which the doctrine of successive phases of feelings
must be examined lies in the ambiguous formulation given
the notion 'propositional feelings.' On the one hand it is
said that "A propositional feeling can arise only in a late
phase of the process of the prehending subject." [33] And on

32. PR, 325. Note also that there is said to be simultaneous origination of the mental and physical pole.
33. "A propositional feeling can arise only in a late phase of the
process of the prehending subject. For it requires, in earlier
phases: *a*) a physical feeling whose objective datum includes the
requisite logical subject; and *β*) a physical feeling involving a
certain eternal object among the determinants of the definiteness of
its datum; and *γ*) the conceptual feeling of this eternal object,
necessarily derivative from the physical feeling under heading (*β*),

the other hand the unity of an incomplete phase is said to be a propositional unity; [34] a thesis which is elaborated in the notion that "Each new phase in the concrescence means the retreat of mere propositional unity before the growing grasp of real unity of feeling" (PR, 343). This side of the theory of propositional feelings is related to subjective aim in one of the formulations of the latter.

> The 'subjective aim,' which controls the becoming of a subject, is that subject feeling a proposition with the subjective form of purpose to realize it in that process of self-creation (PR, 37).

Something of the spirit of this definition is seen in the further comment on 'propositional unity,' namely, that "Each successive propositional phase is a lure to the creation of feelings which promote its realization" (PR, 343). Here a proposition is a lure for feeling; [35] and the subjective aim is an aim at the incorporation of that lure into realization. It is important for the present train of thought that even an early phase possesses "a conceptual feeling of subjective aim" (PR, 342).

It will be profitable to seize upon this notion of 'realization' for a moment, as it is important in understanding what Whitehead must mean by a 'phase.' If realization is here thought of as integration with the physical pole, the ambiguous status of propositional feelings becomes at least a little clearer, since we can then interpret propositional feeling as the whole root of a process—that which is necessary to integrate the physical pole with other feelings—and still think of it as a kind of feeling which itself can be integrated with the physical pole in a "later" phase. This suggestion requires that we once more recur to the notion of succession as having meaning only when viewed from the physical pole. Phases are successively *realized* according to categoreal condition IV; and *perhaps* (δ), some conceptual feeling which is a reversion from the former conceptual feeling, according to categoreal condition V, involving another eternal object as its datum" (PR, 397).

34. PR, 342.
35. The meaningfulness of this notion in the present connection is criticized in chapter 3, pp. 115–18.

because from the point of view of the physical pole there is successive integration of it with other feelings. From the point of view of the mental pole there are no phases, and, in so far as the subjective aim is thought of as belonging to the mental pole, the proposition felt by the subject "with the subjective form of purpose to realize it in that process of self-creation" must be thought of as a proposition embracing all the phases from beginning to end.[36]

It also appears that however little subjective intensity a new actual entity may have, however little novelty it adds, the phases in which in another entity novelty might be important appear to be present. There are many passages that ascribe mere conformity, or negligible novelty, not to the *absence* of the various components of the supplemental phase, but to their *triviality*.[37] This is, after all, what we should expect, because the analysis of successive phases is the analysis of the growth of the physical pole by way of the action of the mental pole, and no actual entity is without its mental pole and therefore none without its freedom from mere conformity.

v.

CONFORMATION AND THE THREE ELEMENTS OF FREEDOM

In chapter 1, I suggested that there are three elements in the factor of freedom, *a)* indetermination; *b)* novelty (sometimes identified with creative *advance* by Whitehead); and *c)* self-causation, in the sense of an aim at a certain subjective intensity of feeling. The general topic of the present sections raises two difficulties for this interpretation.

The first of these has to do with the sense—discussed briefly in chapter 1—in which freedom admits of degree. The factor of freedom is to be found in any actual entity, but in some the freedom is trivial and in others it is of immense importance. There are three senses of "degree

36. The problems that this raises about the reality of the modification of subjective aim, and therefore the reality of self-causation, are dealt with in chapter 3.
37. E.g., PR, 325.

of freedom," which correspond roughly to the three elements of freedom just mentioned. There is first of all the degree of freedom *available* to an actual entity, this being measured by the character of the conditions it departs from. This corresponds to the element of novelty (b) in the sense that conditions may permit more or less novelty. Second, there is the degree of freedom *chosen* by the actual entity, within the limits of what is available to it. This corresponds to the sense in which self-causation is an aim not necessarily at a *maximum* of subjective intensity but at a *certain* subjective intensity (c). To choose anything less than the greatest possible intensity is to exhibit more conformity and less freedom. Finally, there is the sense of freedom in which the entity is *absolutely* free to choose anything up to the maximum intensity afforded by its conditions, and this corresponds to (a) the element of indetermination.

It is perhaps odd to stretch the notion "degree of freedom" to include this last sense. But the point at issue is nevertheless of some importance. One may put it another way by saying that the first two senses of degree of freedom concern the degree to which self-causation is dominant over inheritance, but that there is also a sense of freedom in which (on Whitehead's hypothesis) there is *absolute* freedom to choose among degrees of self-causation. It appears, then, that actual entities must be *absolutely free* to choose among several *degrees of freedom;* so that, an entity once complete, we might be able to say that it has exercised less freedom than it could have done.

The subjective intensity actually chosen (element c) is nothing more than a measure, in terms of feeling, of an actual entity's contribution to its own status. God, then, is the measure of freedom because he is, as we shall see, the absolute standard of intensity, or 'formal immediacy' of feeling. And consequently negligible intensity is thought of as negligible freedom. Elements (a) and (b) of the factor of freedom are given in such passages as the following.

what becomes involves *repetition* transformed into novel *immediacy* (PR, 207).

> The feeling is always novel in reference to its data; since its subjective form, though it must always have reproductive reference to the data, is not wholly determined by them (PR, 355).

> in each concrescence whatever is determinable is determined, but . . . there is always a remainder for the decision of the subject-superject of that concrescence (PR, 41).

Whitehead's remarks on the *absence* of novelty [38] make it quite clear that he thinks novelty necessary for any *heightening* of subjective intensity.

> Apart from the intervention of God, there could be nothing new in the world, and no order in the world. The course of creation would be a dead level of ineffectiveness, with all balance and intensity progressively excluded by the cross currents of incompatibility. The novel hybrid feelings derived from God, with the derivative sympathetic conceptual valuations, are the foundations of progress (PR, 377).

But while it is true that novelty is a necessary condition for enhancement of intensity, and also true that each novelty has its own intensity, it is not true that each novelty is a sufficient condition for a heightening of intensity. God utilizes order and novelty, having intensification as his end, but order and novelty are but means to that end,[39] and sometimes the means do not produce the desired results. Novelty may be fortunate or disastrous,[40] and

---

38. 'Novelty' is here taken only in reference to the world of extensive actual entities; there is no novelty in God.

39. "God is the organ of novelty, aiming at intensification" (PR, 104). " 'Order' and 'novelty' are but the instruments of his subjective aim which is the intensification of 'formal immediacy' " (PR, 135). "God is indifferent alike to preservation and to novelty. He cares not whether an immediate occasion be old or new, so far as concerns derivation from its ancestry. His aim for it is depth of satisfaction. . . . Thus God's purpose in the creative advance is the evocation of intensities. The evocation of societies is purely subsidiary to this absolute end" (PR, 160–61).

40. PR, 410, 284.

the best that can be brought out of a given *impasse* may be bad.[41]

But in talking of novelty we come to our second difficulty, namely, the problems surrounding the topic of conformation. We have noticed that novelty is necessary to subjective intensity of feeling; but, as we shall see in section E, where the discussion is in terms of order, the environment of a given actual entity may be thought of as consisting of layers, with more uniformity in the proximate than in the remote layers. Thus an actual entity whose subjective form contains consciousness will usually have inherited with some directness from another entity containing consciousness, and less directly from other actual entities in which little more than, say, the transmission of energy will be exemplified. Now where there is a high degree of conformation, little subjective intensity is said to be involved. Seemingly then, there is a correlation between lack of novelty and lack of subjective intensity. We should thus expect an actual entity which contains consciousness, but which yet conforms in important respects to its most immediate predecessor (which might also be a conscious actual entity), to have no more intensity than some actual entity exemplifying merely the transmission of energy, and conforming in a like degree to *its* background.

But certainly Whitehead intends us to understand that the actual entity containing consciousness is far higher in freedom and in its subjective intensity than the actual entity exemplifying mere transmission of energy. In one sense the problem is readily solved by always judging the intensity of an actual entity in relation to the actual world taken in general (or perhaps in relation to the lowest order prevailing in the actual world) rather than in relation to the immediate background to which an entity might conform in important respects.

But even if we should so solve the problem of subjective intensity, what would be the position if we were to

41. PR, 373.

find some 'routes' of inheritance in which successors would exhibit *complete* conformity to predecessors, and would therefore have intensities equal to those of the predecessors? Should we then have the element of inde-termination? And should we have any novelty, except in relation perhaps to the *average* of the environment?

In the first place Whitehead seems to doubt whether this complete conformation is possible.

> In considering the life-history of occasions, forming the historic route of an enduring physical object . . . the satisfactions of the antecedent occasions may be uniform with each other, and each internally without discord or incitement to novelty. In such a case, apart from novel discordance introduced by the environment, there is the mere conformal transformation of the feeling belonging to the datum into the identical feeling belonging to the immediate subject. Such pure conformation involves the exclusion of all the contraries involved in the lure, with their various grades of proximity and remoteness. This is an absolute extreme of undifferentiated endurance, of which we have no direct evidence (PR, 285).

If we set aside the *degree* of intensity involved in any actual entity, we might observe that to speak of a *subjective* intensity, in Whitehead's system, is always to speak of a *new subject;* and in this new subject what—at the least—is new is a feeling of the universe from a point of view distinct (at least as to the extensive elements) from any other actual entity. Thus *subjective* intensity defines 'novelty' in a minimal way, and stands with it over against *complete* conformation.

On such a view, what Whitehead calls here "mere conformal transformation of the feeling belonging to the datum into the identical feeling belonging to the immedi-ate subject" is not really *mere conformation,* but rather, the transfer of an *equal* (or almost equal) *intensity* with *maximum* conformation. That there is any subjective in-tensity at all, i.e. feeling belonging to an 'immediate sub-ject,' means that we are dealing with a new entity, with its own indetermination. The point is that 'subject' and 'subjective intensity' are inseparable, and incompatible with complete conformation. Of course even in the passage quoted Whitehead allows for a sense in which the conformity would not be complete, when he speaks of conformation "apart from novel discordance introduced by the environment"; and we should need nothing more to insure that we are dealing with a subject with some subjective intensity.

The whole point here is that although intensity always involves contrasts rather than a dismissal of incompatibilities, the contrasts involved in any new entity may be conceivably of no higher order than those involved in an immediate predecessor. Novelty and subjective intensity require each other, but novelty need not mean *heightened* intensity. Complete conformity is therefore a myth, so that of any actual entity we may always say

A]   It exhibits *some* novelty and *some* subjective intensity, and is at least indeterminate as to whether it is to reproduce *precisely* the same intensity.

B]   In reference to its *immediate* background,

    1) novelty is usually not great, but *may* be in certain special cases;

    2) novelty and intensity may be negligible, the former often so, the latter only when the actual entities composing the immediate background are themselves of negligible intensity;

    3) there may be novelty without *heightening* of intensity; and there may be a decline in intensity.

C]   In reference to its *broadest* background, or to its background *in general,*

    1) novelty and intensity may both of them range upward from the negligible;

    2) there is usually, but not necessarily, a heightening of intensity.

It must be kept in mind throughout this whole account that the idea of indetermination must be preserved in order to make the account of freedom intelligible. Thus, when we say that any actual entity has some subjective intensity (and therefore at least a minimal degree of novelty), we must also say that the new actual entity is not *determined* to the same intensity as its immediate predecessor. It may be that the route of occasions of which it is a part will not permit to the new entity more intensity than, say, its immediate predecessor in the route; but the new entity must be thought of as able to choose slightly less. A more likely situation is one in which a route of occasions exhibits a certain average of intensity, with little variation from a mean; in such a case the new actual entity might be thought of as indeterminate in the sense that it is able to choose slightly more or slightly less than its immediate predecessor, with the "average" viewed as a statistical look backward.

I do not mean to suggest that the foregoing account is to be found in any systematic way in Whitehead. In particular, I have not found any distinction made, with immediate pertinence to the problem of freedom, between conformation to an immediate and conformation to a more remote environment. There seems to be no system-atic presentation of the relations between 'novelty,' 'intensity,' and 'intensification,' and one sometimes gets the impression that self-causation always involves not just intensity, but intensification as well.[42] No doubt some of these passages include the aim of God in their scope.

> This 'aim at contrast' is the expression of the ultimate creative purpose that each unification shall achieve some maximum depth of intensity of feeling, subject to the conditions of its concrescence (PR, 381).

The indetermination of an actual occasion might allow it to thwart this purpose. Other passages do not fit this pattern, and seem to express the view that a new entity always involves a heightened intensity.

> In every instance for which we can analyse, however imperfectly, the formal constitutions of successive occasions, these constitutions are characterized by contraries

---

42. See PR, 165, where the passage "Each actuality is essentially bipolar [with] . . . a conceptual reaction . . . partly introductory of, a relevant novel contrast," could be interpreted to mean that each actual entity exhibits an increased intensity of feeling.

supervening upon the aboriginal data, but with a regular-
ity of alternation which procures stability in the life-
history. Contrast is thus gained. In physical science, this is
'vibration' (PR, 285).

Added contrast should, by the definition of intensity,
heighten it; but it is hard to think of a vibratory phenomenon as constantly growing in intensity of feeling. Perhaps
we can, although I am sure without much warrant in the
text, interpret vibration as a variation, upward and down-
ward, of intensity of feeling.[43]

However much we may fail of finding the three elements of freedom consistent at all points with Whitehead's various discussions, they represent a kind of bare
scheme of his theory of freedom. The major difficulty will
perhaps continue to reside in the relations between 'conformation,' 'subjective intensity,' and 'degree of freedom.'
Though any actual entity exhibits both efficient causation
and final causation—or self-causation, and therefore, by
definition, freedom—there always remains the question
how to interpret the efficient causation. It does not seem
possible that, if we should choose to think of degree of
freedom as equivalent to degree of subjective intensity,
we can avoid the fact that the efficient causation (in the
case of an entity springing from a society of high intensity) plays an important part in a high degree of subjective intensity. Possibly such difficulties are not to be
avoided if we include in a theory of freedom more than
the bare notion of indetermination.

D.
'Subjective form' | 'datum for feeling'

Our discussion will again be directed both towards the
explanation of these two ideas as examples of the opposition of the factor of freedom and the factor of condition

43. There is at least some warrant for this interpretation, since
Whitehead then goes on (PR, 285–86) to interpret a phenomenon of
growth in terms of increased subjective intensity, and one of decay
in terms of decrease of subjective intensity.

and towards the further elaboration of the doctrine of feeling, which is perhaps the central notion in Whitehead's metaphysics. For the latter purpose, 'subjective form' will be examined in greater detail than 'datum for feeling'; the latter notion will receive only such treatment as is needed to make the contrast clear and to furnish an appropriate background for chapters 5 and 6, where ideas related to 'datum for feeling' receive considerable development.

Whitehead states the relation of the expressions 'subjective form' and 'datum for feeling' in a way that makes a convenient starting point.

> The breath of feeling which creates a new individual fact has an origination not wholly traceable to the mere data. It conforms to the data, in that it feels the data. But the *how* of feeling, though it is germane to the data, is not fully determined by the data. The relevant feeling is not settled, as to its inclusions or exclusions of 'subjective form,' by the data about which the feeling is concerned. The concrescent process is the elimination of these indeterminations of subjective forms. The quality of feeling has to be definite in respect to the eternal objects with which feeling clothes itself in its self-definition. It is a mode of ingression of eternal objects into the actual occasion (PR, 131).

A datum is that which is a potentiality for being a component in a feeling, and the term is therefore synonymous with the notion 'object.' [44] An object, or datum, is something perfectly determinate and complete, but indeterminate as to the precise mode in which it will find inclusion in some other actuality. The terms 'potentiality,' 'datum,' and 'object' therefore apply to the same thing. The prototype of the datum—in the sense of something determinate in itself but indeterminate as to its inclusion—is the eternal object. The status as datum of any entity other than an eternal object can therefore perhaps be shown to depend upon the status belonging to eternal objects. This aspect of the problem is reserved for chapters 5 and 6; here we

44. PR, 136.

may treat a datum, or an object, as anything whatever that has definiteness, can be felt, and is indeterminate as to how it is to be felt, without going into the matter of the source of its definiteness.

With this in mind it can be said that "The 'settlement' that an actual entity 'finds' is its datum" (PR, 227). The formulation here is not very precise: the datum is 'decided' by the settled world, or it is the 'real potentiality,' provided by the settled world, but it is not clear whether we are dealing with a situation just *before* the start of a new entity, just *at* the start of a new entity, or just *after* the start of a new entity. Whitehead makes himself clearer by a distinction between 'initial datum' and 'objective datum,'[45] a distinction which is, as has been noticed, virtually the same as the one between 'actual world' and 'objectification.'[46] The initial datum is a settled world given to an actual entity, but in abstraction from the perspective from which the actual entity starts;[47] the objective datum is a selection from the initial datum, which selection "is the way in which the antecedent universe enters into the constitution of the entity in question, so as to constitute the basis of its nascent individuality" (PR, 230). This is the sense in which data "are not extrinsic to the entity" (PR, 304). The point to be noticed in connection with subjective form is that neither the initial datum nor the objective datum can wholly settle the subjective forms of the feelings in which they are felt, although "whatever be the freedom of feeling arising in the concrescence, there can be no transgression of the limitations of capacity inherent in the datum" (PR, 168).

Subjective form is so described as to make it seem precisely what makes a feeling a feeling. It is called 'private matter of fact,'[48] or the 'how' of a feeling,[49] and may therefore be thought of as the factor that permits one to speak of an actuality as a subject-superject rather than as merely a superject.

45. PR, 230, 337–38.
46. PR, 356.
47. PR, 338.

In the analysis of a feeling, whatever presents itself as also *ante rem* is a datum, whatever presents itself as exclusively *in re* is subjective form, whatever presents itself *in re* and *post rem* is 'subject-superject' (PR, 355–56).

I have said that the notion of superject expresses the aspect of an actual entity that justifies our calling it a togetherness of other entities. The notion of subjective form now adds to that togetherness an interior quality in virtue of which the togetherness is not a *mere* togetherness, but rather one properly spoken of as a *feeling*.[50] There are difficulties here, but I shall defer treatment of them for the moment in favor of continuing the exposition so that the contrast with 'datum for feeling' shall more effectively appear.

Subjective form is the source of novelty in the concrescence of an actual entity because it is that by which there is transformation of a datum into an element in a *feeling*. The following passage treats of other actual entities only, but it is easily generalized to include eternal objects.

> The 'prehension' of one actual entity by another actual entity is the complete transaction, analysable into the objectification of the former entity as one of the data for the latter, and into the fully clothed feeling whereby the datum is absorbed into the subjective satisfaction— 'clothed' with the various elements of its 'subjective form' (PR, 82).

In this clothing of the datum, there are certain things held in common in the datum and in the subjective form, and certain elements that are novel in the subjective form.

> Further, the subjective form cannot be absolutely disjoined from the pattern of the objective datum. Some elements of the subjective form can be thus disjoined; and they form the subjective form as in abstraction from the patterns of the objective datum. But the full subjective

48. PR, 32.
49. PR, 338.
50. But see the earlier discussion of 'contrast.'

> form cannot be abstracted from the pattern of the objec-
> tive datum. . . . Also the subjective form, amid its own
> original elements, always involves reproduction of the pat-
> tern of the objective datum (PR, 356–57).

The reader will remember the two-way functioning of eternal objects, by which in the conformal phase of feeling they constitute elements of the definiteness of the datum and elements of the definiteness of the subjective form. The principle is here laid down that this two-way functioning does not tell the whole story of subjective form, for "creativity, universal throughout actuality, is characterized by the datum from the past; and [immanent decision] [51] meets this dead datum—universalized into a character of creativity—by the vivifying novelty of subjective form selected from the multiplicity of pure potentiality" (PR, 249). The data may serve other feelings with other subjects, but the subjective form embodies the novelty of just *this* concrescence.[52]

The difficulties in the relation between the novelty introduced in a subjective form and the subjective intensity of the actual entity have been discussed in the previous section. The intimate connection between the two is noticed by Whitehead when he makes the point that it is only by an abstraction that the qualitative and quantitative aspects of a subjective form are separable from each other and from the character of the datum.

> It is true that there is an abstract qualitative pattern, and
> an abstract intensive pattern; but in the fused pattern the
> abstract qualitative pattern lends itself to the intensities,
> and the abstract intensive pattern lends itself to the quali-
> ties (PR, 356).

> Also, though we can discern three patterns, namely, the
> pattern of the datum, the pattern of emotional quality [of
> the subjective form], and the pattern of emotional inten-
> sity [of the subjective form], we cannot analyse either of

51. See chapter 3, pp. 118–20.
52. PR, 354.

the latter patterns in complete separation from the pattern of the datum, or from each other (PR, 358).

Just why the qualitative and quantitative sides of subjective form should be inseparable becomes apparent at once if the role of eternal objects is kept in mind. If we focus attention only on the qualitative aspect of subjective form, we find it depends upon a qualitative pattern derived from the old entity, and upon just how other eternal objects are used in an integration with this derived qualitative pattern.[53] Here 'how' an eternal object is used means with just what other eternal objects it is combined and in just what way, so that 'pattern,' 'how,' and 'qualitative' get at the same thing. And if we then turn to the problem of intensity, we find that, both in the derivative and originative aspects of subjective form, it also depends upon a certain kind of togetherness of eternal objects, the difference being that intensity depends upon the *number* of eternal objects held in a given feeling as contrasts felt without incompatibility. Any qualitative pattern is as much a pattern as any other, but the patterns differ in richness. The intensive and qualitative side of a subjective form are therefore inseparable: if intensity is increased or diminished, new eternal objects must be added, or some must be taken away. This produces a change in just how eternal objects are together in the subjective form, and thus brings about a qualitative change. Moreover the qualitative pattern to which addition is made already contains intensities as part of it.

> For the relative intensities of the qualitative elements in the qualitative pattern are among the relational factors that constitute that qualitative pattern (PR, 356).[54]

53. PR, 368.
54. In List III of the Corigenda for *Process and Reality* published in *Alfred North Whitehead: Essays on His Philosophy*, ed. George L. Kline (Englewood Cliffs, New Jersey: Prentice Hall, 1963) the following remark is made about this passage. "Many readers have thought that some of the instances of 'qualitative' should read 'quantitative.' We now agree that this passage is probably correct as it stands" (p. 205). I also agree, and my interpretation is of course consistent with this reading.

A discussion of the functioning of eternal objects in the subjective form of a feeling offers an opportunity for the development of the distinction—already noticed—between eternal objects of the objective species and those of the subjective species.[55] An eternal object of the objective species can only obtain ingression as an element in the definiteness of some datum, either a nexus or some single actual entity; it can never be an element in a subjective form. An eternal object of the subjective species is a "determinate way in which a feeling can feel. It is an emotion, or an intensity, or an adversion, or an aversion, or a pleasure, or a pain" (PR, 446). It is not restricted to this functioning, but can also be an element by which one actual entity is objectified in another.

> In this way, the eternal object which contributes to the definiteness of A's feeling becomes an eternal object contributing to the definiteness of A as an objective datum in B's prehension of A. The eternal object can then function both subjectively and relatively (PR, 446).

It will be obvious that in discussing subjective form we have been dealing only with eternal objects of the subjective species, which have both their qualitative and quantitative functioning, and which bring about conformal feelings by way of their two-way functioning. It has been our point that some are derived from earlier entities and some are novel. And it is eternal objects of the subjective species that Whitehead has in mind when he says that "The subjective form in abstraction from the feeling is merely a complex eternal object" (PR, 356). We have in fact been making such an abstraction, since we are talking about the definiteness of a subjective form where that definiteness is a complex eternal object having a qualitative and an intensive aspect. There remains the question in just what sense one abstracts from the feeling when he deals with subjective form as we have been doing.

It does seem that Whitehead, in abandoning the notion of a subject that feels, is constrained to describe that which feels as a mere togetherness of feelings; whereupon a feeling itself becomes a kind of ontological ultimate.

> for the philosophy of organism, the subject emerges from the world—a 'superject' rather than a 'subject.' The word 'object' thus means an entity which is a potentiality for being a component in feeling; and the word 'subject' means the entity constituted by the process of feeling, and including this process. The feeler is the unity emergent from its own feelings; and feelings are the details of the process intermediary between this unity and its many data (PR, 135–36).

But this is not all, for when one examines the feeling he finds that it too appears to be a togetherness of components—the components this time being eternal objects. As I hope to have shown in the earlier remarks on contrasts,[56] togetherness in a feeling, although not a mere disjunction, since the unity is a genuine synthesis of the diverse elements, appears to be ultimately the togetherness of certain kinds of eternal objects, having internal relations as regards their relational essences.[57] This depletion of the notion 'feeling' of all common reference is only evaded by declaring the component eternal objects to be together 'in a feeling.' Perhaps it is inevitable that a feeling should appear mysterious once the feeler is rejected except as the 'unity emergent from its own feelings.' In any case I submit that in the following passage 'subjective form inhering in feeling' is at least as mysterious as 'quality inhering in a particular substance,' which Whitehead would have it replace.

> The fundamental example of the notion 'quality inhering in a particular substance' is afforded by 'subjective form inhering in feeling.' If we abstract the form from the feeling, we are left with an eternal object as the remnant of subjective form (PR, 354).

Especially is this so when one learns that the description of the feeler as the 'unity emergent from its feelings' is

56. See section CIII of this chapter.
57. See also chapters 5 and 6.

qualified by ascribing that unity to subjective aim, which is (in one formulation) the feeling of a proposition with a certain subjective form; for this of course makes the unity of the feeler depend upon one of the component feelings.

All this seems to remove the perhaps mysterious notion of a substantival entity—with all its attendant problems having to do with internal relations—only to supply its place by an even more mysterious ultimate. I would here suggest that, if one looks for something besides a subjective form (in the sense of a complex eternal object) in one of these feelings, he will find only a vector character. This complex of eternal objects *here* contains a vector character to other complexes of eternal objects out *there*.

It now remains to develop the earlier suggestion that even this vector character is dependent upon eternal objects, this time of the objective species. They represent the element in Whitehead's philosophy by which he intends to avoid the idea of an infinite regress of feelings and therefore of internal relations.

> Thus a member of this species can only function relationally: by a necessity of its nature it is introducing one actual entity, or nexus, into the real internal constitution of another actual entity. Its sole avocation is to be an agent in objectification. It can never be an element in the definiteness of a subjective form. The solidarity of the world rests upon the incurable objectivity of this species of eternal objects. . . . This is a real physical fact, with its physical consequences. Eternal objects of the objective species are the mathematical platonic forms. They concern the world as a medium (PR, 445–46).

In the light of this, these eternal objects are at once revealed as not internal to feeling, and as *therefore* rendering possible, as an outward referent, the internality of feeling. This status becomes clearer when it is seen that the very possibility of extensive connection depends upon these external objects.

> The order of nature, prevalent in the cosmic epoch in question, exhibits itself as a morphological scheme involving eternal objects of the objective species. The most

fundamental elements in this scheme are those eternal objects in terms of which the general principles of coordinate division itself are expressed. These eternal objects express the theory of extension in its most general aspect (PR, 447–48).

A vector is not possible unless entities, however internally related, are in some sense outside each other, and this is what the extensive scheme—given in terms of eternal objects of the objective species—takes account of.

> It is by means of 'extension' that the bonds between prehensions take on the dual aspect of internal relations, which are yet in a sense external relations. It is evident that if the solidarity of the physical world is to be relevant to the description of its individual actualities, it can only be by reason of the fundamental internality of the relations in question. On the other hand, if the individual discreteness of the actualities is to have its weight, there must be an aspect in these relationships from which they can be conceived as external, that is, as bonds between divided things. The extensive scheme serves this double purpose (PR, 470–71).

The reader need hardly be reminded that the extensive connection here under discussion is given by the coordinate rather than genetic division of the satisfaction. Indeed all the doctrine of objective eternal objects asserts is that the coordinate analysis of the satisfaction of an actual entity does not yield *only* feelings. Besides the feeling revealed there is a definiteness, given in terms of eternal objects of the objective species, which expresses the place of the actual entity in a space-time continuum—its extensive region. This definiteness is what causes it to be felt vectorally.[58]

58. It should be noted that the eternal objects of the objective species that form part of the definiteness of an actual entity *A*, while they do not enter into the subjective form of an actual entity *B* that feels *A*, none the less enter into the definiteness *B* has as an object for some later entity *C*. Eternal objects of the objective species are thus "passed along" from entity to entity, but may undergo changes in the process because of the way in which they are felt, and because of the perspective of the new entity. In *Adventures of Ideas*

If this interpretation is reasonably correct, it is fair to suggest that feelings and eternal objects are the basic elements in Whitehead's philosophy, and that, because the datum of the feeling, the character of the extensive relation to the datum, and the internality of the feeling are all given in terms of eternal objects, the latter are more ultimate ontologically than are the feelings. The significant point here is that where the regress of internal relations (between actual entities other than God) is broken, it is broken by eternal objects. This matter is discussed at length in chapters 5 and 6.

This section can be brought to a close with a brief discussion of the confusion that sometimes seems to exist in the relation between 'subjective form' and 'subjective aim.' I have noticed that subjective aim, in one of its

(p. 286 ff.) the difference between the eternal objects of the objective species exemplified in A and those exemplified in B is called the difference between 'reality' and 'appearance.' "The distinction between 'appearance' and 'reality' is grounded upon the process of self-formation of each actual occasion. The objective content of the initial phase of reception is the real antecedent world as given for that occasion. This is the 'reality' from which that creative advance starts. . . . The intermediate phase of self-formation is a ferment of qualitative valuation . . . the initial objective content is still there. But it is overlaid by and intermixed with the novel hybrid prehensions derived from integration with the conceptual ferment. . . . The mental pole has derived its objective content alike by abstraction from the physical pole and by the immanence of the basic Eros which endows with agency all ideal possibilities. . . . *This difference between the objective content of the initial phase of the physical pole and the objective content of the final phase, after the integration of physical and mental poles, constitutes 'appearance' for that occasion. In other words, 'appearance' is the effect of the activity of the mental pole, whereby the qualities and coordinations of the given physical world undergo transformation*" (AI, pp. 269–70; italics supplied). It is obvious that the transmission of energy discussed earlier (section CIV) involves the transmission of eternal objects of the objective species with unimportant change. "In respect to the occasions which compose the societies of inorganic bodies or of the so-called empty spaces, there is no reason to believe that in any important way the mental activities depart from functionings which are strictly conformal to those inherent in the objective datum of the first phase. . . . There is no effective 'appearance' " (AI, p. 271). With the applications of the doctrine of 'appearance' and 'reality' to the matter of perception we are not here concerned.

formulations, is the subject feeling a proposition with the subjective form of realizing it in that concrescence; but it now seems that subjective forms are dependent on subjective aim.

> The emotional pattern in the subjective form of any one feeling arises from the subjective aim dominating the entire concrescent process (PR, 420).

Not only the subjective form of a single feeling but also the relations among the subjective forms of all the feelings of a given actual entity are dominated by the subjective aim.

> Also prehensions are not independent of each other. The relation between their subjective forms is constituted by the one subjective aim which guides their formation. This correlation of subjective forms is termed 'the mutual sensitivity of prehensions . . .' (PR, 359).

This is of course another way of saying that the mental pole dominates the character of feelings.

> The concrescence is dominated by a subjective aim which essentially concerns the creature as a final superject. This subjective aim is this subject itself determining its own self-creation as one creature. Thus the subjective aim does not share in this [genetic] divisibility. If we confine attention to prehensions concerned with the earlier half, their subjective forms have arisen from nothing. For the subjective aim which belongs to the whole is now excluded. . . .
> The summary statement of this discussion is, that the mental pole determines the subjective forms and that this pole is inseparable from the total *res vera* (PR, 108).

The present concern is with subjective form as opposed to datum for feeling, and any possible inconsistency in the relation between subjective form and subjective aim is therefore reserved for chapter 3. It should be plain, though, that the present chapter leads up to the problem of the exact status of subjective aim, a problem which involves the antithesis of an indivisible mental pole and a development or process thought of as a self-creation. The status of subjective aim is the key to the question whether self-creation is a doctrine sustained by the rest of Whitehead's philosophy.

E.
'Objective lure', 'lure for feeling', 'real potentiality' | 'actual world', 'the given'

In the present contrast we are concerned not so much with the actual entity considered as having both a factor of freedom and a factor of condition as with the factor of condition itself. We shall consider it on the one hand as a determinate limitation—that which *must* be felt by an actual entity; and on the other hand as indeterminate by affording alternatives—that which may be felt in *alternative ways*. That which is given to an actual entity may impose an almost complete conformation or may give it a wide scope for its own free development.

As a preliminary, the term 'object' may be defined more precisely than I have so far defined it. Any entity—actual entity, eternal object, proposition, or whatever—that intervenes "in processes transcending itself, is said to be functioning as an 'object' " (pr, 336). Such intervention is a functioning as a datum for feeling, and in this sense objects are 'potentials for feeling.'[59] But once again the notion 'potential' has both a determinate and an indeterminate side: the object is what it is, but it may be felt in various ways. This is quite clear as touching eternal objects, which are by definition determinate in the sense of 'definite,' but less clear in connection with actual entities, which are in process. But an actual entity, when its concrescence is finished, or satisfied, is a "definite, determinate, settled fact, stubborn and with unavoidable consequences," and in this role it does intervene "in processes transcending itself" and can therefore be thought of as an 'object.' It is always an element of an actual entity as satisfied that is prehended.

Borrowing Descartes' terminology, Whitehead says

59. pr, 136, 366.

that when we speak of the satisfaction of an actual entity we have regard to its existence *objectivé* [60] and can then speak of it as 'objectively immortal.' And, borrowing from Locke (with what justification I need not attempt to decide), he speaks of the 'power' exerted by an actual entity in its existence *objectivé*. Here once again the question of something determinate in itself, indeterminate as to its utilization arises. In its existence *objectivé, a)* an actual entity is definite and settled, and *b)* it can be utilized in many ways. Of course we may also *c)* look at a specific instance of its use. The term 'power' is evidently used to cover all three senses; thus, the following passage deals with (*c*).

> Locke adumbrates . . . the principle that the 'power' of one actual entity on the other is simply how the former is objectified in the constitution of the other (PR, 91).

Senses (*a*) and (*b*) are dealt with as follows.

> The terminal unity of operation, here called the 'satisfaction,' embodies what the actual entity is beyond itself. In Locke's phraseology, the 'powers' of the actual entity are discovered in the analysis of the satisfaction (PR, 335).

Of course all that has been said about powers can also be applied to eternal objects, which are perfectly determinate, and yet are indeterminate as to how they shall be felt.[61]

60. PR, 336. Whitehead's point in using this word is clear enough, but it should be observed that Descartes uses the word to characterize one aspect of *ideas:* the objective reality of an idea is its character as representing some reality for us. If there is a real thing correspondent to the idea, then that real thing is, in Descartes' terminology, a *subjective* (or formal) reality: it possesses, that is, the reality of a subject. For Descartes all realities whatsoever—men, stones, thinking substances, and ideas (which he took to be *modes* of thinking substance)—had each of them its own subjective reality. Ideas, on the other hand, were unique in *also* possessing an objective, or representative, reality. The note of settled, finished, and concrete actuality that Whitehead intends by the word *objectivé* is then not present in Descartes' use of the word.

61. In chapters 5 and 6 the notion of 'power' as applied to an actual entity is held to be derivative from the fact that the actual entity receives its definiteness from the ingression of eternal objects.

If one were to consider the realm of eternal objects in abstraction from all actual entities whatever, this realm (taken together with "mere" creativity) would then be called 'boundless, abstract possibility' or a 'bare inefficient disjunction'; one would then find that it utterly lacked the 'relevance' needed by a lure for feeling. For this realm to become a 'real potentiality' the (objective) intervention of actual entities is needed.

> This objective intervention of other entities constitutes the creative character which conditions the concrescence in question. The satisfaction of each actual entity is an element in the givenness of the universe: it limits boundless, abstract possibility into the particular real potentiality from which each novel concrescence originates. The 'boundless, abstract possibility' means the creativity considered solely in reference to the possibilities of the intervention of eternal objects, and in abstraction from the objective intervention of actual entities belonging to any definite actual world, including God among the actualities abstracted from (PR, 336–37).

Whitehead wishes to make the point that a potentiality is a lure for feeling and, to emphasize the function of other actual entities in making the potentiality a real one, he speaks of real potentiality as the 'objective lure.' [62]

> The 'objective lure' is that discrimination among eternal objects introduced into the universe by the real internal constitutions of the actual occasions forming the datum of the concrescence under review (PR, 281).

Here it is plain that there are two ways of applying the term 'objective lure.' *a)* Any actual world can be thought of as the settled outcome of the functioning of the finished actual entities that form it. If we attend to the way in which this functioning has so qualified the realm of *eternal objects* as to affect the way in which they are to be felt by some new actual entity to which this actual world belongs, we can designate *real potentiality* as the objective lure. *b)* But we can also seize upon the fact that it is

62. Cf. chapter 3, pp. 115–18.

just *this* actual world, consisting of just *these* actual entities, that is to be felt by the new actual entity. In this case,
having it in mind that these *actual entities* are indeterminate as to *how* they are to be felt, we may speak of *them,*
rather than the realm of eternal objects they have qualified, as the objective lure. The point depends upon the
interdependence of forms and actual entities—an interdependence that Whitehead insists upon by calling the eternal objects 'forms of definiteness' of actual entities.

The 'lure for feeling' is a more special notion and is
introduced here partly because it affords a convenient
way of introducing the functioning of God's 'primordial
nature,' by means of which God forms part of the actual
world of any actual entity. The lure for feeling is the
selection from the objective lure that is admitted into
'subjective efficiency.' [63]

> The 'lure for feeling' is the final cause guiding the
> concrescence of feelings. By this concrescence the multi-
> fold datum of the primary phase is gathered into the unity
> of the final satisfaction of feeling (PR, 281).

Sometimes when speaking rather loosely Whitehead
seems to identify 'subjective aim' and 'lure for feeling,' [64]
but here his sense seems to be that the lure for feeling is
the 'ideal of itself' at which the subjective aim of an actual
entity aims.[65] The relevance of God's primordial nature
here becomes apparent, for it is God in his primordial
nature that establishes the initial lure for feeling of an
actual entity, by conferring upon it its initial subjective
aim. Now if we forget for a moment the problem of how
an initial subjective aim becomes the final or full subjective aim of an actual entity—a very crucial problem indeed—we can say that a lure for feeling emerges out of an
objective lure precisely because God is one of the mem-

63. PR, 133.
64. PR, 130. This present discussion is expository rather than critical; the appropriateness of identifying 'subjective aim' and 'lure for
feeling' is questioned in chapter 3, and the consistency of Whitehead's
use of the term 'lure' is there criticized.
65. PR, 130, 133.

bers of the objective lure: the reader will remember that the actual world of any actual entity always includes God. This fact is otherwise expressed by saying that the initial subjective aim of an actual entity is the result of its feeling the primordial nature of God with a 'hybrid' physical feeling.

> the primary phase of a temporal actual entity is physical. . . . A 'physical feeling' is here defined to be the feeling of another actuality. If the other actuality be objectified by its conceptual feelings, the physical feeling of the subject in question is termed 'hybrid.' Thus the primary phase is a hybrid physical feeling of God, in respect to God's conceptual feeling which is immediately relevant to the universe 'given' for that concrescence. There is then, according to the category of conceptual valuation, i.e. Categoreal Obligation IV, a derived conceptual feeling which reproduces for the subject the data and valuation of God's conceptual feeling. This conceptual feeling is the initial conceptual aim referred to in the preceding statement. In this sense, God can be termed the creator of each temporal actual entity (PR, 343).[66]

There is here the singular circumstance that God's function as principle of concretion is to cause a hybrid physical feeling of himself to emerge out of a situation 'riddled with ambiguity.' No clearer example of the deontologizing character of Whitehead's metaphysics of feeling could be asked for. The principle of concretion does not bring about a new entity, properly speaking; it rather brings about a certain kind of feeling, of such a character that other feelings are simultaneously brought about in a concrescence, or growing together, with it.

But perhaps the deepest question to be asked here is whether the lure for feeling, or subjective ideal of itself, aimed at by the subjective aim of an actual entity does not negate the character of the objective lure, from which it is said to be a selection. Does not the indetermination of the

---

66. For the sense in which the initial subjective aim is the result of the objectification of God in an actual entity, see PR, 46.

objective lure vanish if the lure for feeling controls, in being a selection from the objective lure, just how that indetermination is to be felt?

The question may be put in a different fashion by asking whether God's role as part of the actual world that qualifies boundless potentiality so as to produce real potentiality does not, from the standpoint of a new actual entity, remove the sense of potentiality entirely, and constitute the mental pole as rather a given element in the new concrescence. Further consideration of this matter will be reserved for chapters 3 and 4. Here, with attention once more to the explicit side of the doctrine, one can say that Whitehead allows for the development of the lure for feeling,[67] or, what comes to the same thing, for modifications in the subjective aim.[68] We shall eventually have to question the validity of the word *lure* in just this connection, but at any rate it is plain that Whitehead wishes to set over against the given character of the actual world a realm of possibility that is not compulsive.

Still with attention to the explicit side, I should like to examine the alleged differences in the richness of objective lures. The question is how some conditions offer more freedom than others—how, that is, the indeterminations afforded by various actual worlds differ in the intensities that can arise from them. Now freedom is something not entirely explicable in terms of the conditions it meets, but a condition is none the less at once a limitation and an opportunity; and opportunities can be more or less momentous. In section Cv it was suggested that the degree of freedom was identical with the degree of subjective

67. "The primary element in the 'lure for feeling' is the subject's prehension of the primordial nature of God. . . . The lure for feeling develops with the concrescent phases of the subject in question" (PR, 287).
68. "Each temporal entity, in one sense, originates from its mental pole, analogously to God himself. It derives from God *its basic conceptual aim, relevant to its actual world, yet with indeterminations awaiting its own decisions. This subjective aim in its successive modifications,* remains the unifying factor governing the successive phases of interplay between physical and conceptual feelings" (PR, 343; italics supplied). Cf. PR, 375.

intensity attained by an actual entity. It can now be added that the momentousness of an opportunity is measured by the degree of freedom, or subjective intensity, it affords. Of course the reservation is made that the freedom of the entity requires that *it* choose its own intensity out of those afforded. Its freedom to choose the highest or lowest afforded lies in the indetermination that is a component of freedom. If, however, it chooses the highest possible, we say it has exercised the highest degree of freedom open to it. And we say this because it has then exhibited less conformity, or is less a product of efficient causes, and is therefore more self-caused. We have already seen the difficulty that arises because a high degree of freedom seems to require *conformation* to an immediate background of high order. It is now necessary to clarify some of the matters left obscure in the earlier discussion in section Cv.

Whitehead offers both a basic notion of order, and a derivative application of this in the theory of 'societies.' The formulation of the basic sense of order that is perhaps most consistent with the doctrine of feeling is the following.

> The degree of order in the datum is measured by the degree of richness in the objective lure (PR, 136).

The 'degree of richness' is here to be identified with 'subjective intensity afforded.' Notice that the subjective intensity *actually aimed at* by a new actual entity does not define the order in the actual world which is its datum: the highest intensity which the actual entity *could aim at* when confronted with this datum defines that order. It does seem, however, that Whitehead does not always keep in mind the requirements of his doctrine of freedom when he explains this doctrine of order, for it sometimes appears that the order *produces* rather than *affords* the subjective intensity. This must be kept in mind in a formulation like the following, where the word 'disorder' can only be a way of calling attention to the fact that there are degrees of order.

The intensity of satisfaction is promoted by the 'order' in the phases from which concrescence arises and through which it passes; it is enfeebled by the 'disorder' (PR, 129–30).

It will at once appear that 'order' and 'disorder' have quite a different sense when we deal with the *derivative* sense of order. The basic sense of order is said to be "primarily applicable to the objective data for individual actual entities"; and as such it is contrasted with another sense of order, which is said to be derivative, and which represents the application of the word to "the relations among themselves enjoyed by many actualities which thereby form a society" (PR, 136). Here the sense in which a society affords intensity for one of its members is not emphasized. It is true that the society is thought of as a low or as a high one, depending on whether its members have high or low intensity. The words 'disorder' and 'order' no longer apply, however, to the intensity afforded but to the degree to which the 'defining characteristic'[69] of a given society is dominant. Now the propagation of a defining characteristic throughout a society is one example of efficient causation, so that order now seems the degree to which such efficient causation is dominant, and disorder the degree to which it fails of dominance.

This runs counter to the freedom inherent in the *basic* notion of order, and occasionally also introduces confusion into the account of the latter. Thus the dominant ideal proper to an actual entity is its subjective aim, which

69. "The members of the society are alike because, by reason of their common character, they impose on other members of the society the conditions which lead to the likeness.

"This likeness consists in the fact that (*i*) a certain element of 'form' is a contributory component to the individual satisfaction of each member of the society; and that (*ii*) the contribution by this element to the objectification of any one member of the society for prehension by other members promotes its analogous reproduction in the satisfactions of those other members. Thus a set of entities is a society (*i*) in virtue of a 'defining characteristic' shared by its members, and (*ii*) in virtue of the presence of the defining characteristic being due to the environment provided by the society itself" (PR, 137).

may be interpreted as the degree of subjective intensity chosen by its 'teleological self-creation' [70] from the richness of the objective lure presented. The dominant ideal is therefore correlated with the basic sense of order, which, however, is defined as we saw by the highest intensity the entity *could* aim at, and not the dominant ideal actually chosen. On the other hand, the dominant ideal of a society is the defining characteristic proper to it, which, as it is propagated, represents order in the derivative sense, and which, in so far as it fails of propagation, bespeaks the presence of disorder.

The confusion is increased by the fact that there is doubtless a connection between the two senses of 'dominant ideal': the dominant ideal of a society is after all determined in part by the subjective aims, dominant ideals, of its individual members, and these individual dominant ideals spring in turn—at least in part—from the 'dominant components' given them by the society. This undoubted connection of the two senses goes back to the interpenetration of environment and individual. The following quotation expresses this interpenetration, and it is easy to see how the sense in which the environment contributes to the actual entity can obscure the sense in which the actual entity contributes to the environment.

> The causal laws which dominate a social environment are the product of the defining characteristic of that society. But the society is only efficient through its individual members. Thus in a society, the members can only exist by reason of the laws which dominate the society, and the laws only come into being by reason of the analogous characters of the members of the society (PR, 139).

This is the sort of situation that leads Whitehead—I think quite without conscious derogation of his doctrine of freedom—to speak of the "dominant ideal peculiar to each actual entity," i.e. its subjective aim at an ideal of itself, as arising from the "dominant components in its phase of 'givenness,'" [71] i.e. from the defining characteristic of the society, in so far as that characteristic is dominant.

70. AI, 256.
71. PR, 128.

To correct this inadvertence—if it is one—one need only think of the defining characteristic of the proximate society within which an entity finds itself, i.e. the dominant components in the given, as simply one element in the richness of the objective lure presented to the actual entity. This preserves freedom in the sense that this objective lure can then legitimately be thought of as a lure and not a compulsion. It is not totally decided for the new actual entity that it will repeat all of the defining characteristic of the society in which it finds itself. It may not exemplify the defining characteristic, and then there will be said to be some disorder in the society—but then it should be remembered that the environment is also dependent on the entity, and that the notion of disorder here represents not only a characteristic of the society presented to the new actual entity, but also the character of the actual entity's choice. And the element of disorder may introduce a higher intensity. Whitehead does not seem to make this clear, but it follows if we are not to make efficient causes entirely decisive. This suggestion could be summarized by saying that the degree of order (in the basic sense) is the highest degree of intensity open to the choice of a given actual entity in virtue of its data; and that the degree of order (in the derivative sense) in the immediate society that is *part* of that data is the degree to which the intensity chosen by the actual entities forming the society is regularized. But the regularization or lack of it would always appear as a function of *a)* the society as presented to an actual entity *and b)* the choice of that actual entity.

This is to insist that the doctrine of societies must always be qualified by the sense in which an actual entity *a)* is a novelty, *b)* contains indetermination, *c)* exhibits self-causation in the sense of an aim at a certain subjective intensity. But it by no means does away with the problem that there may be a high degree of conformation to a proximate society, and that this is generally correlated with efficient causation and therefore with conformal feelings and a lack of intensity. Thus note that the following description of the inheritance of a defining characteristic is quite consistent with the picture of the dominance of efficient causation.

> A nexus enjoys 'social order' when   i] there is a common element of form illustrated in the definiteness of each of its included actual entities, and   ii] this common element of form arises in each member of the nexus by reason of the conditions imposed upon it by its prehensions of some other members of the nexus, and   iii] these prehensions impose that condition of reproduction by reason of their inclusion of positive feelings involving that common form. Such a nexus is called a 'society,' and the common form is the 'defining characteristic' of that society. (AI, 261; the passage is there quoted from PR, part I, chapter III, section II, where, however, "of that" is found instead of "involving," in the last sentence but one; the later form presumably represents a correction of Whitehead's.)

"Explanation by 'tradition,'" Whitehead has said, "is merely another phraseology for explanation by 'efficient cause.'" [72] And, speaking of a society that is highly ordered (has a defining characteristic that is quite dominant), he has implied that there would be "the shackle of reiteration from the past." [73] In general the description of the situation in which there is a high degree of order (derivative sense) in a society is much like the description he gives of conformal feelings. I do not think we can entirely resolve the difficulties here. There is indeed a partial resolution—to be dealt with later—based on the fact that escape from the shackle of one kind of order, with the aim of attaining an order exhibiting higher intensity, is by way of the disorder found together with the first order. I have tried to show that this disorder must be given in terms not only of the settled elements in a society, but also in terms of the decision of any actual entity confronted with these settled elements. But besides this resolution, the fact must be faced that an actual entity may conform to its immediate society, and yet, when that society manifests a high degree of experient intensity on

72. PR, 159.
73. PR, 161.

the part of its members, may have a high degree of subjective intensity anyway.

The interpretation I offer to account for this turns on
what efficient causation consists in for an entity described
entirely in terms of feelings. *What* is felt is an efficient
cause; if it is the feeling of another actual entity, then it
enters into the feeler; if it is an eternal object of the
objective species, it does not enter into the feeling but
enters somehow into what the feeler leaves behind *it* as
objective. But if we take an efficient cause as a component
in the total definiteness of the feeler, then, the more
efficient causes there are, the less efficient causation is
dominant. It will be remembered that self-causation, or
teleological self-creation, consists in the integrating of
components in contrasts that might otherwise be incompatibilities, so that the more things a feeler is able to conform to, the less conformation it exhibits. Thus if we ask
what is conformed to when an actual entity conforms to
the defining characteristic of a society that offers a rich
objective lure, the answer is that there is conformation to
a "dominant definition of compatible contrasts" (PR, 142).
This seems merely the abrogation of conformity to just a
few elements among many "thwarting, contrary decisions
. . ." (PR, 142) in favor of conformation to a whole host of
elements, held in effective contrasts.[74] There is thus perhaps a lack of clarity in Whitehead's notion of conformation, in that it often seems to be the *opposite* of subjective
intensity. If this is not necessarily so, it is a mistake for
Whitehead to say flatly that there is negligible autonomous energy where conformal feelings predominate. The
intensity prevailing in the society to which conformation
is made must always be considered.

It may be that difficulties of this kind are due to the
presence of another sense of freedom, not taken account

74. My point might be expressed by saying that the more conformation (in the sense of dominance of conformal feelings) there is, the
fewer elements are conformed to in the sense of being felt in
effective contrast; while the more origination there is, the more a
large number of elements are conformed to in the sense of being felt
in effective contrast.

of in the three characteristics (novelty, indetermination, self-causation) I have listed. Thus, though Whitehead is careful to say that the freedom in the universe can
give rise to an intensity less than the best available to it,
he sometimes, as in the above comment on the 'shackle of
reiteration,' seems to say that freedom requires an *advance* in intensity over the intensity achieved by the actual entities in the datum. I have no doubt that in speaking of freedom Whitehead sometimes has this sense of
freedom in mind. Whether or not this is an inadvertence
on his part, it is certain that, even on the doctrine I have
been expounding, *advance* in intensity is an *advance* in
freedom. We may say that however shackled an actual
entity is by its environment it is none the less free with the
degree of freedom equivalent to the intensity of other
members of that society; but it will still be true that if a
new actual entity is to show an *increase* of freedom, it
must show an increase in intensity. Now both degree of
freedom, and enhancement of a degree of freedom, are
dependent upon the 'capacity inherent in the datum.'

> The character of an actual entity is finally governed by
> its datum; whatever be the freedom of feeling arising in
> the concrescence, there can be no transgression of the
> limitations of capacity inherent in the datum. The datum
> both limits and supplies (PR, 168).

It now remains to be noticed that the richness of the
datum, i.e. of the objective lure, which richness is what we
mean by the basic sense of order, requires the derivative
sense of order and disorder, since there must be some
dominance of societies, with the reservation that this dominance must be only partial. That "The dominance of
societies, harmoniously requiring each other, is the essential condition for depth of satisfaction" (PR, 142), is a
thought expanded as follows.

> Apart from the reiteration gained from its societies, an
> environment does not provide for the massiveness of em-
> phasis capable of dismissing its contrary elements into
> negative prehensions. Any ideal of depth of satisfaction,

arising from the combination of narrowness and width, can only be achieved through adequate order (PR, 169).

But the dominance of a given society must be partial if there is to be not only intensity, but also advance in intensity.

> There are various types of order, and some of them provide more trivial satisfaction than do others. Thus, if there is to be progress beyond limited ideals, the course of history by way of escape must venture along the borders of chaos in its substitution of higher for lower types of order (PR, 169).

Of course it goes without saying that Whitehead does believe that the 'persuasive' effort of the primordial nature of God, or the 'Eros' [75] of the universe will assure that the course of history will be generally upward, i.e. that in some extensive actual entities there will appear a gradual heightening of subjective intensity. It is one of the difficulties of Whitehead's doctrine of freedom that along a given route of actual entities there is not *always* a gain of freedom—and this simply because of the *freedom* actual entities have. This kind of paradox arises because, while the degree of freedom an actual entity has is measured by the freedom of God, the doctrine of responsibility requires that God's functioning shall not be compulsive for actual entities. And it is apparently to this end that indetermination and novelty, no less than a subjective aim at a certain intensity, form part of the notion of freedom as that concerns extensive actual entities. Whitehead must explain why, however rich the lure extended, it need not be wholly taken, and he must not explain the refusal of the best alternative by the compulsiveness of another alternative in the environment.

Thus, whatever the inconsistencies we may have uncovered, it is necessary to think of the environment with its quota of dominant and partially dominant societies (order and disorder in the derivative sense) as constituting only an objective *lure* of a given richness (degree of

75. This identification is made at AI, 326; also *passim*, as indexed.

order in the basic sense, with disorder now complementary only in the sense that the term points to the possibility of a lesser degree of richness). By definition a lure exercises persuasion but no compulsion. In chapter 4 a criticism of the doctrine of creativity calls this explicit doctrine in question.

Summary and anticipation

It will be recalled that the purpose of this chapter was to set forth the explicit doctrine, interpreting inconsistencies where possible, and only to indicate the direction criticism would take. *In the summary the expository side is not considered;* instead, an attempt is made to give the main points that emerge as relevant to the later criticism.

The actual entity was considered as a concrescence, or growing together, of feelings [76] which aim at the feeler. Because a feeling is an internal relation of the feeler to other actual entities and eternal objects, the whole internal constitution of an actual entity is given by such relations. But in its own self-causation the actual entity chooses in part the feelings it will enter into; and it does this by means of one of its feelings, which dominates the concrescence as a subjective aim at subjective intensity. The autonomy of this aim becomes important only in the supplemental phases of the concrescence.

The reality of the phases of an entity's development was questioned   *a)* because of the epochal theory of time, which seems to make succession a matter that concerns only the physical pole; and   *b)* because, while propositional feelings are said to arise in a late phase, subjective aim, which seems to be present in any phase of the development, is in one formulation spoken of as the feeling of a proposition. Because of these considerations self-causation in terms of modification of subjective aim through successive phases will have to be examined.

---

76. Despite its failure of application in the case of negative prehensions, the word *feeling* will be used instead of prehension, as offering a more immediate connection with common speech.

Later developments were adumbrated in the suggestion that a feeling, or even a togetherness of feelings, might be thought of as a certain kind of togetherness of eternal objects. Four factors were important: *a)* the definiteness of a physical feeling is given by eternal objects; *b)* the subjectivity of a feeling seems to be defined by a complex eternal object of the subjective species; *c)* the vector referent of a physical feeling seems to be given by eternal objects of the objective species; *d)* in a contrast, or unity of components as felt, the definiteness of the components is given by eternal objects and their unity by the internal relations among the component eternal objects (as to their relational essences). The result is that the internal relations of a "feeler" to "felt" elements disappear in favor of internal relations among the "felt" elements.

3

The Criticism:

Subjective Aim

Introduction

WE MAY CONVENIENTLY take as our starting point those remarks in the first chapter in which 'self-causation' (or 'self-creation'), 'subjective aim,' and 'final causation' were said to be equivalent, and simply different ways of describing the factor of freedom. I made the reservation that all these terms must be taken as consistent with the sense of freedom embodied in the phrase "the final reaction of the self-creative unity of the universe." Whitehead claims that this reaction is beyond all the determinations that partly form it. He does not therefore wish us to identify subjective aim as factor of freedom with subjective aim as a determinate component in a concrescence. It is the purpose of this chapter and the following one to determine whether Whitehead's exposition of subjective aim, self-causation, and final causation, really sustains these conditions. If it does not there will be some grounds for thinking of an actual entity as a function of two perfectly determinate elements: an actual world exercising efficient causation, and a God described in terms of a static valuation of eternal objects. It is absolutely necessary to Whitehead's theory of freedom that he sustain the doctrine that "however far the sphere of efficient causation be pushed in the determination of components of a concrescence—its data, its emotions, its appreciations, its purposes, its phases of subjective aim—beyond the determination of these components there always remains the final reaction of the self-creative unity of the universe" (PR, 75). To decide whether this doctrine is sustained we shall have to examine both the topic of subjective aim and in the next chapter that of creativity. The latter topic will afford us another attack on the question what Whitehead means by 'actual entity.' We shall eventually maintain that the sense in which an entity is a superject dominates in Whitehead's doctrine the sense in which it is a subject. We shall also hold that the sense in which an entity is a superject is the sense in which it is at any stage a togetherness of determinate components. This consideration depends upon the criticism of Whitehead's doctrine of self-causation to which this chapter and the next are devoted.

There are two basic problems in connection with subjective aim. The first is that of the conflict between subjective aim considered as an indivisible unity belonging to the whole of the actual entity, and the same subjective aim considered as undergoing successive modifications. The second is that of the nature of these modifications and their relation to self-causation. The second problem does not of course arise unless we so resolve the first as to permit some sense in which subjective aim is really modified. I shall turn to the first problem in the following section and to the second problem in the succeeding ones.

Subjective aim: modification or indivisible unity?

In chapter 2 there was some discussion of the contrast between the successiveness exhibited by—as it seemed—the physical pole, and the indivisibility of the mental pole; the connection of this contrast with the epochal theory of time was also mentioned. It was there argued that, on the basis of the indivisibility of the mental pole, one would not expect to find any successiveness in subjective aim. And because Whitehead quite clearly held that there *were* successive modifications of subjective aim, it was suggested that there was at least an apparent contradiction. It is now necessary to go into this apparent contradiction in greater detail, and to make more precise the solution to it that was adumbrated in the second chapter.

Before touching again on the connection with the epochal theory of time, another sense of the unity of subjective aim may be developed. The sense in which subjective aim gives unity to a set of feelings is expressed by Whitehead both in terms of the subjective forms of the feelings, and in terms of the feelings themselves; in the latter case the data of the feelings is also kept in mind. In the first case Whitehead speaks of the relation between the subjective forms as "constituted by the one subjective aim which guides their formation (PR, 357). In the second case he speaks of the "mutual sensitivity of the feelings in one subject," which expresses "the notion of final causation in the guise of a pre-established harmony" (PR, 338). These principles are embodied in the first and the seventh Categoreal Obligations—the Category of Subjective Unity, and the Category of Subjective Harmony;[1] it will be sufficient to cite the first.

> The many feelings which belong to an incomplete phase in the process of an actual entity, though unintegrated by reason of the incompleteness of the phase, are compatible for integration by reason of the unity of their subject (PR, 39).[2]

The two categories enunciate the pre-established harmony that is the "outcome of the fact that no prehension can be considered in abstraction from its subject, although it originates in the process creative of the subject" (PR, 41).

This doctrine of a pre-established harmony, coupled with the claim that the unity of a concrescence is at any moment incomplete because of the presence in an actual

1. PR, 40–41.
2. See also PR, 341–42.

entity of what Alexander has called a "principle of un-rest," [3] returns us at once to the sense in which the mental pole is indivisible. Where the unity of incomplete feelings is their capacity for integration in a subsequent phase; where this is given by the subjective aim; and where the subjective aim belongs to an actual entity that involves a principle of unrest; it must follow that the full unity of the actual entity must be given in terms of the subjective aim for the full period of concrescence. In terms of the pre-established harmony, if there is such a harmony at any phase we choose, then there must be one for the whole entity, in the sense that the subjective aim is always *for* the whole entity.

Turning to the character of the entity's contribution to physical time, we consider again the connection of the theory of the indivisible unity of subjective aim with the epochal theory of time. It was stated earlier that the provision for the unity and indivisibility of subjective aim was apparently related to the requirement that although time forms a continuum as a background, it is not contin-uous in its growth. Whitehead stresses this when he says that "the act of becoming [of the creature] is not exten-sive," although "in every act of becoming there is the becoming of something with temporal succession" (PR, 107). Now if this were the only connection of the problem of the indivisible unity of subjective aim with the epochal theory of time, a possible solution to our present problem would be open to us. We could take the formula to mean that any of the 'durations' or 'arrests' in which time grows is not itself in time but, taken with other atomic durations, makes time. The act of becoming would not then be extensive. It could still, however, be a development of a sort, and we might take subjective aim to develop with it, as part of the whole 'pattern' that is said, in *Science and the Modern World*,[4] to require a duration which must be

3. PR, 43.
4. "But the potential pattern requires a duration; and the duration must be exhibited as an epochal whole, by the realisation of the pattern. Thus time is the succession of elements in themselves divisible and contiguous. . . . Temporalisation is realisation. Tem-

exhibited as an 'epochal whole.' We should then be dealing with a development that is not a temporal one in the
sense that it characterizes a duration that contributes to
time without being *in* time. No doubt it is not a very clear
solution, but it is at least consonant with Whitehead's
usual terminology.

But this is not all Whitehead means, as he makes clear
when he says that "subjective aim does not share in this
(genetic) divisibility . . . the mental pole determines the
subjective forms and . . . is inseparable from the total *res
vera*" (PR, 108); or again, that "Every actual entity is 'in
time' so far as its physical pole is concerned, and is 'out of
time' so far as its mental pole is concerned. It is the union
of two worlds, namely, the temporal world and the world
of autonomous valuation" [5] (PR, 380). Plainly he means
not only that the growth of the pattern is in a duration
rather than in time, but also that the subjective aim, or
mental pole, in that it controls the development of that
pattern, does not itself belong to the development. It
would then appear that the mental pole is the source of
the epochal character of time, because it is the source of
the atomic character of actual entities. We have not
merely the problem that there is no time within the development of an entity; we must also deal with the source of
the claim that "the genetic growth . . . is undivided" (PR,
435), because we are concerned with what makes an
actual entity atomic.

Since in the present section we are only concerned

poralisation is not another continuous process. It is an atomic
succession. Thus time is atomic (i.e. epochal), though what is
temporalised is divisible" (SMW, 179). The thought that this atomic
growth is also the growth of the space element of extensiveness is
given as follows, ". . . a duration is spatialised; and by 'spatialised'
is meant that the duration is the field for the realised pattern
constituting the character of the event" (SMW, 177). ". . . [an]
organism is an event holding in its essence its spatio-temporal
relations . . . throughout the spatio-temporal continuum" (SMW,
180).

5. As I noticed in chapter 2, there is an inadvertence here in speaking of the physical pole as in time; it would be more in keeping
with his theory to say, as he does in fact say elsewhere, that the
genetic growth is not in time but contributes some of its features
to physical time. See PR, 434.

with the problem whether modification of the subjective aim can *in any sense* be compatible with this unity and indivisibility, it is only necessary at this point to say that there are numerous passages in which the modification of subjective aim during genetic development is insisted upon.[6] There is plainly a conflict of some sort.

If this conflict is to be resolved at all, the resolution must come by an examination of the sense in which an actual entity has both an element of process and an element that is exempt from process. In the earlier account I attempted to explain this paradox by saying that the "phases" of the mental pole resulted merely from looking at the mental pole from the point of view of the physical pole. This is an unsatisfactory explanation in that it not only suggests that the "modifications" of the mental pole are illusory, but also expresses a tendency to hypostatize the physical and mental poles, and then to talk of their integration. What is valuable in this earlier explanation must be retained without making the entity appear as a composite of two discrete poles.

The two important and in a sense conflicting elements can be more subtly phrased: *a)* the act of 'valuation,' or 'envisagement' or 'conceptual feeling,' is a feeling that is nonextensive while still furnishing the pivot upon which process turns; *b)* the other feelings of an actual entity exhibit a development, in the sense that the entity embodies a principle of unrest. We must think of an actual entity as an indissoluble unity of a "temporal world and a world of autonomous valuation." It at once appears that there is then no contradiction in thinking of the whole actual entity as at once divisible and indivisible: if the epochal theory of time makes sense, then this also makes sense. The modification concerns the divisibility, and the unity

6. "This basic conceptual feeling [i.e. conceptual feeling of subjective aim] suffers simplification in the successive phases of concrescence" (PR, 342). "This subjective aim, in its successive modifications, remains the unifying factor governing the successive phases of interplay between physical and conceptual feelings" (PR, 343). "It [the process of concrescence] is finally responsible for the decision by which any lure for feeling is admitted to efficiency (PR, 135).

of subjective aim concerns the indivisibility. The difficulty really lies in showing how modification in the divisible element of the entity is also a modification in the indivisible element without detracting from the unity and indivisibility of the latter.

The only acceptable solution, I think, is to say that while the actual entity taken as a concrescence of feelings exhibits extensiveness, one element in the concrescence must always be a feeling that *a) concerns the whole development of the concrescence,* and *b)* does not have as its datum any extensive actual entity. The act of valuation then is always found to be inseparable from a phase of process, but is always a valuation *for* the whole process. It is thus an indivisible unity although it is one of the feelings in a divisible process. Valuation for Whitehead is always exempt from passage, as we can see very clearly in his description of God as a valuation of eternal objects; but in this case any phase reflects its limitations back into the valuation.

Now this does give us a sense in which the subjective aim is both an indivisible unity and modified; and if it seems a dark saying, it is at any rate no darker than the claim that an actual entity is the unity of a "temporal world and a world of autonomous valuation." But the question remains whether one side of the interpretation does not swallow the other. If we take the indivisibility and unity of the subjective aim to mean *merely* that the subjective aim is always the unifying factor of the actual entity and always for the whole, then perhaps there is no problem. But if we add that the subjective aim is nonextensive, then it is hard to see how the actual entity as a whole can *really* modify the subjective aim, and we are led to suspect that "modification" merely expresses the sense in which the actual entity in its extensive feelings can never, in any one *phase* of the feelings, embrace the whole of the indivisible nonextensive feeling that guides it. "Can an indivisible *really* be modified?" is simply the question whether in an actual entity involving both a process and an eternal valuation, the process is real. Here "real" means effective, active, able to change matters; and not simply a real absorption of the ideal that controls it.

Now I think that at just this point, and almost at the outset of our investigation of subjective aim, there is very good reason to call this theory a radical finalism. The matter is inconclusive in the sense that Whitehead does not give us a statement of the indivisibility of subjective aim that is clear enough for us to say it is without doubt in contradiction to the idea of the efficacy of process in modifying subjective aim. No doubt too, many of his remarks on the indivisibility of subjective aim reflect a concern to make clear the epochal theory of time, in which a whole extensive region is actualized as one quantum under the guidance of an aim which has as its concern that whole quantum. It may be that by the indivisibility of subjective aim, by its unity, and by its exemption from extensiveness as well, he means only that subjective aim is always a unity of feeling reflecting concern for the whole entity—but a whole entity that any moment of the process is still indeterminate as to just what its *whole* concrescence will be, and *therefore* indeterminate as to the whole of the aim that is to guide it.

We seem at this point to have a choice among three alternatives: *a)* rejecting Whitehead's theory as a radical finalism, on the ground that the modification is in the process but not in the ideal that controls the process; *b)* ignoring the nonextensiveness and indivisibility of subjective aim as an imperfectly digested remnant of the epochal theory of time; *c)* accepting the paradox that modification is possible in an act that is nonextensive because the act is the act of an actual entity that is also extensive. Acceptance of the last alternative involves interpreting the nonextensiveness of subjective aim as merely equivalent to its being an aim directed towards the whole of an entity. And acceptance of either (*b*) or (*c*) involves taking the concrescence of an actual entity seriously. Obviously Whitehead wishes us to do this, and, since the evidence for (*a*) is inconclusive, I shall accept the notion of the modification of subjective aim as at any rate not incompatible with the unity of the mental pole on the grounds so far stated. The rest of the account of subjective aim forms an attempt to show its place in a concrescence of feelings. When the charge of radical finalism is again brought, it will be brought on grounds that involve the determinateness of the components in a concrescence, and the relation of such determinateness to the doctrine of creativity.

The place of subjective aim in the concrescence

Subjective aim is the final cause of the concrescence of an actual entity, yet it takes its start from a hybrid physical feeling of God, which is an example of efficient causation; it is the end or ideal of an actual entity, yet is not fully present in an entity until its concrescence is ended; it is that which makes the feelings of the entity what they are, yet it is itself a feeling in the composition of the actual entity; finally it is sometimes described as a feeling and sometimes as the ideal which is felt. The terminology used in describing it is not always consistent, and it is sometimes metaphorical. This is understandable, since in this doctrine Whitehead seeks to make clear the very motility of creativity, a concept which is as ultimate as any in his philosophy. Accordingly, we should not do well to look for the same nicety and consistency of technical usage we might demand in some of the more peripheral of his notions. But some of the ways in which subjective aim is discussed are clearer than others and more closely interwoven with the rest of his technical terminology. In what follows I shall try to keep steadily in mind the setting of an actual entity that is a concrescence of feelings and shall always bring the exposition of subjective aim back to it.

There are four points that are of particular importance. *a)* Subjective aim is an element in a concrescence of feelings and is therefore one of the component feelings. *b)* It is the feeling in the actual entity that controls and unifies the other feelings. Its concern is thus with the whole of the concrescence, and thus although it is the principle of unrest itself it is exempt from the process, in the sense already questioned. *c)* But the controlling feelings and the controlled feelings are separable only abstractly: the subjective aim is the unity of the feelings, but *this* subjective aim requires *these* feelings to be what it is. *d)* As any feeling is a feeling of some datum, a subjective aim has a datum of its own, namely, a proposition.

Two passages express these points with especial clarity. The first I have cited before.

> The 'subjective aim,' which controls the becoming of a subject is that subject feeling a proposition with the subjective form of purpose to realize it in that process of self-creation (PR, 37).

> The determinate unity of an actual entity is bound together by the final causation towards an ideal progressively defined by its progressive relation to the determinations and indeterminations of the datum. The ideal, itself felt, defines what 'self' shall arise from the datum; and the ideal is also an element in the self which thus arises (PR, 228).

The first quotation wears a more technical air than do most of Whitehead's remarks on subjective aim; this is perhaps because it can easily be connected with his theory of propositions, which he gives such extended development. Unfortunately he does not enlarge upon this way of describing subjective aim, except to say that the unity of an incomplete phase of an entity's concrescence is always a propositional unity.[7] This can be taken to mean either that it is a propositional unity because the feeling of a certain proposition gives it its unity, or that the proposition which, in being felt, gives it its unity, is a proposition *about,* among other things, the whole of the entity in question. In the latter case, the entity itself, in its incompleteness, is an element in the complex that, being felt,

7. See chapter 2, section CIV.

constitutes the unity of the process by which the completion of the entity is brought about. The connection with the second quotation lies in the fact that we can then take "ideal" as a "felt proposition," and go on to reword that quotation by saying that "the proposition, itself felt, defines what self shall arise from the datum; and the proposition is also an element in the self which thus arises." By a similar procedure, "the retreat of mere propositional unity before the growing grasp of real unity" (PR, 347) is seen to be identical with "final causation towards an ideal progressively defined by its progressive relation to the determinations and indeterminations of the datum." The passages cited are then easily related to one like the following.

> This basic conceptual feeling [of conceptual aim] suffers simplification in the successive phases of the concrescence. It starts with conditioned alternatives, and by successive decisions is reduced to coherence (PR, 342).

The whole account so far can be related very easily to the doctrine of the subject-superject. In the very strictest sense, a thing is a superject when considered in the light of its satisfaction—the satisfaction being that which is a resultant of the process, settled, determinate, and 'objectively immortal.' Now the satisfaction is the entity as concrete, but it can never form part of the entity as in its concrescence.

> No actual entity can be conscious of its own satisfaction; for such knowledge would be a component in the process, and would thereby alter the satisfaction (PR, 130).

Nevertheless the ideal that guides the concrescence, its propositional unity, is an ideal of the entity taken as a satisfaction, or strict superject.

> In its self-creation the actual entity is guided by its ideal of itself as individual satisfaction and as transcendent creator. The enjoyment of this ideal is the 'subjective aim,' by reason of which the actual entity is a determinate process (PR, 130).

But this 'ideal of itself as individual satisfaction' is no more identical with final satisfaction than the 'basic conceptual feeling' with 'conditioned alternatives' is identical with this same ideal when successive decisions have 're-duced it to coherence.' Thus the sense in which an entity is at any moment subject-superject is identical with the sense in which there is always an ideal present, but always one that is progressively defined. If we attend to the fact that the ideal is an element in a private feeling, we speak of the subject; if we attend to the fact that the entity, taken at any one stage and including the ideal as present in that stage, is something partially 'coherent' and *a result of* the process, we call it a superject.[8] This is the meaning of Whitehead's remark that "at any stage any entity is subject-superject."

Although the ideal of itself entertained at any point by the subject is not identical with what its satisfaction will be, it is nevertheless an ideal of itself *as a satisfaction.* Since the superject is identical with the final coherence reached, i.e. with the satisfaction, Whitehead can therefore claim that "the superject is already present as a condition, determining how each feeling conducts its process" (PR, 341). Thus at any stage of its development an actual entity is subject-superject, and in its private character entertains an ideal of itself as *final* superject, or satisfaction.

From one point of view it is the purpose of this chapter and the next to determine whether the actual entity as subject really progressively defines the ideal "by its progressive relation to the determinations and indeterminations of the datum," or whether it is the determinations and indeterminations of the datum as interacting with determinations and indeterminations of the ideal, that *constitute* the subject. The latter alternative gives a sense in which 'superject' at all times describes the entity more accurately than 'subject' does, and Whitehead often seems

8. "An actual entity is at once the subject experiencing and the superject of its experiences. . . . 'subject' is always to be construed as an abbreviation of 'subject-superject.' " (PR, 43).

to recognize that, and gives priority to the former term.[9]

Although in the preceding section I recognized many difficulties in Whitehead's doctrine of the modification of subjective aim, I conceded the reality of that modification in order to pursue further Whitehead's views on its nature. The discussion in the present section rests upon that concession. We have not yet, however, come to close grips with the question whether this modification can be explained in terms of the interaction of determinate components or must indeed be recognized as a "final reaction of the self-creative unity of the universe." The following section and the next chapter take up these problems.

The nature of the modification of subjective aim

To ask what exactly Whitehead means by the modification of subjective aim is to ask what exactly he means by self-causation. There appear to be two ways in which self-causation may be understood. 1] Self-causation might be the reaction on one another of all the determinate components of the entity. By an actual entity we should then mean merely the sum of its components, and by the gradual envisagement of the ideal, or the gradual reduction of it to coherence, we should mean merely the interaction of the ideal as it is at the beginning with the physical feelings as they are at the beginning. This inter-

9. Note especially, ". . . for the philosophy of organism, the subject emerges from the world—a 'superject' rather than a 'subject.' . . . the feeler is the unity emergent from its own feelings; and feelings are the details of the process intermediary between this unity and its many data" (PR, 135–36).
"The term 'subject' has been retained because in this sense [the sense in which a set of feelings has a unity] it is familiar in philosophy. But it is misleading. The term 'superject' would be better. The subject-superject is the purpose of the process originating the feelings. The feelings are inseparable from the end at which they aim; and this end is the feeler. . . . The feelings are what they are in order that their subject may be what it is" (PR, 339). " 'subject' is always construed as an abbreviation of 'subject-superject' " (PR, 43).

action in turn can also be interpreted in two ways. *a)* Determinate physical feelings, in being integrated with determinate conceptual feelings, both alter the conceptual feelings and are themselves altered. The unity and indivisibility of the conceptual feelings is then simply the fact that they concern the whole concrescence of the actual entity. *b)* Initial subjective aim is a timeless valuation but is general in that it embraces a whole scale of values with alternatives among them. This determinate but general valuation is integrated with the determinate physical feelings with which it is correlated, and then "suffers simplification in the successive phases of the concrescence . . . and by successive decisions is reduced to coherence" (PR, 342). Both [1 a] and [1 b] are not radical finalisms in the sense that the process is guided by a determinate ideal exterior to it and unaltered by it. But the process can be thought of as the product of the interaction of two perfectly determinate factors: an ideal and a set of physical feelings or efficient causes—a kind of mixture of radical finalism and radical mechanism.

[2] Self-causation, on the other hand, although starting with given conceptual and physical components might mean more than the mere interaction of these components. Over and above these components (taking subjective aim in any given phase as a component) self-causation might be an active power indeterminate as to its exercise, capable of choosing arbitrarily among the entities to be felt and contributing to the way in which they are felt. This active power would then be one way of expressing the self-creative unity of the universe. On this view one of the component determinate feelings is the initial subjective aim, and the actual entity in its self-causation freely chooses other elements to become part of their subjective aim and to be integrated with the physical feelings. These elements are not in any sense functions of the other elements that the actual entity must feel by virtue of decisions other than its own, and they do not come from the physical pole.

In the following account an attempt will be made to

show how meanings (*1*) and (*2*) lie side by side in much of Whitehead's exposition of subjective aim. At times there seems a conflict in intention, the same conflict that can be seen in the use of the two terms *subject* and *superject.* The one intention seems to require a self or a subject that, though inseparable from its feelings, can not be explained as only a complex of feelings "thrown up" by the process; the other intention, less concerned with the problem of freedom and more concerned with combatting the substantiality of a subject with a 'vacuous actuality' distinct from all its relations, emphasizes the superjective side of the actual entity.

We shall now investigate the two interpretations by discussing subjective aim in terms of A] lure for feeling, B] originative decision, C] elimination of indetermination, and D] the distinction between initial subjective aim and subjective aim taken without qualification, or, as I have chosen to call it, "full" or "final" subjective aim.

A] The discussion of subjective aim in terms of lure for feeling, must presuppose, if the word 'lure' is to have any meaning, a conception of self-causation in terms of a freedom that is beyond any determination of components. A cause considered as a compulsive determinant can hardly be called a lure. The earlier discussion of lure for feeling [10] will not be repeated, but attention must be called again to certain verbal difficulties. It is first of all remarkable that subjective aim itself is spoken of as a lure for feeling,[11] for the word 'lure' would seem to belong not so much to the aim as to what it is directed upon. Yet even here the word is questionable, since the goal of the aim would seem to be what Whitehead calls the 'subjective ideal,' [12] and this subjective ideal, being at any moment a proposition [13] felt with "the subjective purpose of realizing

---

10. See chapter 2, section E.
11. "The subjective aim is not primarily intellectual—it is the lure for feeling" (PR, 130).
12. PR, 133.
13. See the discussion of propositions in connection with the 'supplemental' phases of feeling, chapter 2, section CIV.

it in that process of self-creation" (PR, 37), does not seem to have the character of a lure; or if it is a lure it seems to be one that has already caught something.

But if one simply accepts the verbal difficulties involved in almost all of Whitehead's explicit remarks on subjective aim, it is not hard to get at the intent of his use of the word 'lure.' This intent appears quite clearly in the discussion of objective lure, for 'objective lure' is another name for real potentiality, and this is clearly capable of being thought of as a lure. Real potentiality is the realm of 'conditioned indetermination,' the eternal objects that make up this realm being conditioned in that they have a relevance to an actual entity and indeterminate in that they can be felt in various ways. The sense in which an actual entity is *causa sui* lies in the originative decision by which elements from this lure are accepted into the reality of conceptual feeling.[14] The following passage makes it quite clear that, in the root sense of "lure," the subjective ideal, or that at which subjective aim is directed, is not a lure but rather that which is selected from the lure.

> The analysis of concrescence, here adopted, conceives that there is an origination of conceptual feeling, admitting or rejecting whatever is apt for feeling by reason of its germaneness to the basic data. The gradation of eternal objects in respect to this germaneness is the 'objective lure' for feeling; the concrescent process admits a selection from this 'objective lure' into subjective efficiency. This is the 'subjective ideal of itself' which guides the process (PR, 133).

If we are to think of subjective aim as identical with self-causation, or self-creation, we must not think of it as the aim at, or entertainment of, an ideal that is at any moment determinate, but rather as the progressive *act* by which an ideal is gradually modified in being entertained. The objective lure, or real potentiality, then becomes the proper correlate of this act, because it is then a realm of the relevantly ideal from which the selection necessary to

14. PR, 131.

the modification is made. It then becomes plain that the term 'subjective aim' is not always a happy one because of a natural association with a teleology conceived more statically than Whitehead intends.

We might, then, take his meaning to be somewhat as follows: 1] there is a lure which is to be identified with the realm of relevant possibilities; [15]   2] an originative feeling in the concrescence of the actual entity makes a selection from this lure;   3] the selection chosen at a given point (if we make an abstraction) is the subjective ideal for that point;   4] subjective aim is to be identified not with the entertainment of a given ideal (for the ideal once entertained is compulsive) but with the progressive and free act of selection of the ideal; in this case the freedom is correlate with the notion 'lure' in [1];   5] we are dealing with aspects of an actual entity that is a unity in process.

In the discussion of 'lure for feeling,' then, if the present interpretation is close to truth, the emphasis is on the successive modifications of the subjective aim rather than on its unity. Also, what is more to our present purpose, the activity belongs *to the concrescence,* and gives a sense in which an actual entity is free, or *causa sui.*

> To be *causa sui* means that the process of concrescence is its own reason for the decision in respect to the qualitative clothing of feelings. It is finally responsible for the decision by which any lure for feeling is admitted to efficiency. The freedom inherent in the universe is constituted by this element of self-causation (PR, 135).

There remains the sense, counter to Whitehead's intention, in which this could be ascribed to a determination by components. Thus the concrescence, in admitting some of the objective lure into subjective efficiency at one stage, does so in part at least because it has in an earlier phase admitted a certain other element of the objective lure into subjective efficiency. This same continuity of process can also be illustrated by reference to subjective forms.

15. See chapter 5, pp. 150–55; and chapter 6, pp. 179–80.

The subjective forms of the prehensions in one phase of the concrescence control the specific integration of prehensions in later phases of that concrescence (PR, 131–32).

A subjective aim—in the sense of the entertainment, rather than the selection, of a subjective ideal—is a feeling with a certain kind of subjective form.

But as we have seen, Whitehead's intentions in this matter are quite clear. There is the insistence that real potentiality is a *lure:* that there is in the realm of eternal objects no compulsive *haecceitas* regulating the growth of any specific actual entity. And there is also the explicit direction that "however far the sphere of efficient causation be pushed in the determination of components of a concrescence—its data, its emotions, its appreciations, its purposes, *its phases of subjective aim*—beyond the determination of these components there always remains the final reaction of the self-creative unity of the universe." [16] But if the intentions are clear, the other account is at any rate quite credible; we have only to think of initial subjective aim as a component, and ascribe its modifications to successive interaction with the physical feelings. And this we should have to do, if there are important elements in Whitehead's doctrine that will not support these intentions.

b] The doctrine that each actual entity has some degree of causal freedom can be summed up in the contention that the given element in history, beyond all rationalization, is the "final accumulation of all . . . decisions—the decision of God's nature and the decisions of all occasions . . ." (PR, 75). In the case of extensive actual entities, such decision is "the final decision of the immediate subject-superject," and constitutes "the ultimate modification of subjective aim." Process is thus thought of as effective, and as elaborating decisions that control its further issue. Whitehead makes a distinction between 'immanent decision,' which is the decision of an extensive actual entity (an actual occa-

16. PR, 75; italics supplied.

sion), and 'transcendent decision,' which is the decision of all actual entities, including the decision of God.

> The immanent decision, whereby there is a supervening of stages in an actual entity, is always the determinant of a process of integration whereby completion is arrived at. . . . This determination originates with conceptual prehensions which enter into integration with the physical prehensions modifying both the data and the subjective forms. . . . Transcendent decision includes God's decision. He is the actual entity in virtue of which the *entire* multiplicity of eternal objects obtains its graded relevance to each stage of concrescence. . . . In 'transcendent decision' there is transition from the past to the immediacy of the present; and in 'immanent decision' there is the process of acquisition of subjective form and the integration of feelings. In this process the creativity, universal throughout actuality, is characterized by the datum from the past; and it meets this dead datum—universalized into a character of creativity—by the vivifying novelty of subjective form selected from the multiplicity of pure potentiality (PR, 248–49).

Transcendent decision only *includes* God's decision; it also includes the decision of all the actual entities making up the actual world of the actual entity whose immanent decision we are concerned with. It thus represents the efficient causality we have already met. Now it would be possible to think of immanent decision as merely the focus of transcendent decision: the product of the decisions of other actual occasions and God, meeting in a node that we call an actual entity. The ultimate consequence of this interpretation would be a reference of all actuality to the decision of God, for we should then be questioning the freedom of all actual occasions and therefore the reality of all the efficient causation said to be exercised by actual occasions. So, for "product of the decisions of other actual occasions and God, meeting in a node," we should have to substitute "product of the *apparent* decisions of other actual occasions and the *real* decision of God, meeting in a node."

Since this is very far from Whitehead's intention, it must also be very far from his intention to think of the modification of subjective aim by way of the simple interaction of components, for such determination by components would be nothing more than the elimination of the *reality* of immanent decision.

Consider, however, the close of the last passage cited. Immanent decision is given in terms of a 'vivifying novelty' meeting the dead datum which already characterizes creativity. This vivifying novelty must come (1) directly from God, or (2) only indirectly from God in his role as *goal* for novelty, and directly from the exercise of an immanent power (over and above the "power" given by God and the 'dead datum') to choose among the alternatives extended by God as organ of novelty. If the latter view is not supported by the nature of creativity, then the former must hold and the doctrine of freedom is indeed merely superimposed on a doctrine that will not bear it. A third alternative, which will be considered in the discussion of the next topic, is that the novelty comes indirectly from God, and is directly the manifestation of a radical and arbitrary origination.

c] The concrescence of an actual entity may be thought of as the 'evaporation' of indetermination: at the outset of the concrescence there is an initial subjective aim given by God, which "constitutes the autonomous subject in its primary phase of feelings with its initial conceptual valuations, and with its initial physical purposes" (PR, 374); but there is an indetermination as to just how the concrescence will then run its course.

> This process of the integration of feeling proceeds until the concrete unity of feeling is obtained. In this concrete unity all indetermination as to the realization of possibilities has been eliminated. The many entities of the universe, including those originating in the concrescence itself, find their respective roles in this final unity. This final unity is termed the 'satisfaction.' The 'satisfaction' is the culmination of the concrescence into a completely determinate matter of fact. *In any of its antecedent stages the*

concrescence exhibits sheer indetermination as to the nexus between its many components (PR, 322–23; italics supplied).

As we asked before whether the immanent decision was real, we can now ask just what it is that brings about the evaporation of this sheer indetermination. This question involves a consideration of the nature of the indetermination. *1*) Is it an indetermination only in the sense that the proposed mixture of two determinate components is indeterminate because it has not yet come into being? If this is the case, then the elimination of indetermination is brought about by the interaction of determinate components, and the indetermination was therefore only apparent.

2) Is there instead a kind of positive indetermination? That is to say, besides the determinate components, which are determinate powers in the sense that felt eternal objects or felt actual entities are powers, is there another indeterminate component, which is a power in another sense? The elimination of indetermination would then come about by way of the intervention of this indeterminate active power. It is necessary to say *active* power here, because an indeterminate static power could not do the job, being mere material for feeling; while a determinate static power would be a determinate component, and, if it intervened to eliminate the indetermination, would give us case (*1*).

Or *3*) are we to take the word 'sheer' at its face value, and say that Whitehead intends that a set of determinate components are indeterminate as to their issue, without there being in the entity any indeterminate power over and above the power exercised by the determinate components (felt elements), and without there being any restriction of 'indeterminate' to sense (*1*). In this case there would be determinately felt actual entities and eternal objects; there would be an indetermination represented by other eternal objects indeterminate as to how they are to be felt; and this indetermination would be eliminated with complete arbitrariness. Here sheer indetermination means simply that the indetermination is eliminated in an arbitrary way, from "nowhere,"—it would not be elimination, as in (2), by an active power, indeterminate as to its exercise, and its own reason for the elimination of this indetermination and therefore of the indetermination of the eternal objects as to how they were to be felt.

Three different ontologies seem in question here. In the first there is an indetermination having merely to do with the interaction of determinates, where the determinates would be given in terms of the determinateness of eternal objects. In the second there is an indetermination peculiar to the entity, an indetermination which makes the concrescence not explicable in terms of interacting determinates. The second interpretation presupposes an indeterminateness that is a *power*, but not a power in the sense proper to an eternal object, or to an actual entity considered in respect of its satisfaction. The third seems to require a radical origination of power; thus the powers in God do not make the choice, the determinate powers that are components in the finite actual entity do not in their interaction entirely make the choice, and above these static powers there seems to be no active power, indeterminate as to its exercise, that makes the choice. The power to resolve the indetermination simply "happens," and the "final self-creative reaction of the universe" would appear to be indistinguishable from chance — chance understood not as a function of our ignorance, but as a radical metaphysical principle. It is an ontology not without precedent in philosophy, but one that is difficult to reconcile with a conception of the individual actual entity as exercising a power *qua* subject.

We must again defer the question which of these ontologies Whitehead is committed to until, in our examination of creativity, we decide whether it has an indeterminateness that can rightly be called that of an active power indeterminate as to its exercise.

D] One of the formulations of initial subjective aim exhibits some of the verbal difficulties that were discussed in connection with objective lure and lure for feeling. In this formulation the initial subjective aim is said to be a prehension of the primordial nature of God, and to be the primary element in the lure for feeling.

> The primary element in the 'lure for feeling' is the subject's prehension of the primordial nature of God. Conceptual feelings are generated, and by integration with physical feelings a subsequent phase of propositional feelings supervenes. The lure for feeling develops with the concrescent phases of the subject in question (PR, 287).

On our earlier interpretation, the lure for feeling is falsely so called. It is really that which is selected from the genuine lure—the genuine lure being the objective lure, or real potentiality. Now God is the major element in the objective lure by establishing the 'proximate relevance' [17] of the realm of eternal objects to each new concrescence. Thus, when a definite prehension of God by an actual entity gives the actual entity its initial subjective aim, it is best to think of this aim as the primary selection from the objective lure. Similarly, instead of saying that the lure for feeling develops, we are more consistent in saying that the subjective ideal develops. Of course the objective lure also develops with the concrescence, because anything that becomes actual and settled puts its stamp on real potentiality as it does so.[18]

This prehension of God's primordial nature by an extensive actual entity is said to be a 'hybrid physical feeling.' That is, God is felt by way of the conceptual feelings he has for the universe given to the concrescence in question.[19] These conceptual feelings can also be thought of as the feelings God has for the *impasse* out of which the actual entity is to rise.[20] God's function as the giver of initial aim is identical with his function as principle of concretion. But in the completion of the concrescence the

17. PR, 73.
18. See chapter 5; chapter 6, pp. 165–85.
19. PR, 343.
20. PR, 373.

actual entity is guided by its 'living'[21] aim, so that al-though God's feeling is the best for that *impasse*, it is intended that it be indeterminate at the start whether the actual entity, as finally constituted in its satisfaction, will be the best that can come out of that *impasse*. The sub-ject-superject is said to be the autonomous master of all but the start of its concrescence. Therefore Whitehead can say that "the mental pole is the subject determining its own ideal of itself by reference to eternal principles of valuation autonomously modified in their application to its own physical objective datum" (PR, 380). Here the phrase 'eternal principles of valuation' designates the ini-tial subjective aim, and the term 'autonomous' insists that the entity itself modifies the valuation.

We should have the answer to the whole of White-head's metaphysics if at this point we could say what he would intend by "the entity itself." The conflict of such a conception (which seems to refer to a *subject*) with Whitehead's ultimate prejudice towards the superject is plain. And so once more one must raise the question whether, if Whitehead were not interested in preserving his doctrine of freedom, the autonomous modification here would not be simply the interaction of these physical feelings with the aim set for them, and whether such an explanation would not cover all the details of his doctrine except the doctrine of freedom. There is a passage that would seem to support such a suggestion.

> whatever is determinable is determined, but . . . there is always a remainder for the decision of the subject-superject of that concrescence. This subject-superject is the universe in that synthesis, and beyond it there is nonentity. This final decision is the *reaction of the unity of the whole to its own internal determination* (PR, p. 41; italics supplied).

The question is whether this reaction of the unity of the whole need be more than the reaction of determinate components in order to satisfy the rest of Whitehead's

21. PR, 373.

doctrine (except the freedom doctrine); and whether there is any sense in which this reaction *could* be beyond the determination of components. The questions just raised in the discussion of the evaporation of indetermination [c above] are pertinent here. Any reaction beyond the determinateness of the components would be an example of either case (2) or case (3), discussed in that place.

THE CRITICISM:

Creativity and *Power*

Creativity

WITHOUT THE DOCTRINE of freedom Whitehead's doctrine becomes a God-centered determinism. Because of the importance given the idea of an eternal and telic pattern of eternal objects, it would be fair to call the result a radical finalism. Whether the doctrine of freedom can stand in its present form and still justify in *any* sense the application of the word 'subject' to actual entities remains a question. To attempt to settle it we now turn to examine his doctrine of creativity. Our investigation will be directed towards an analysis of the locus and nature of power in Whitehead's philosophy, and it will therefore not be completed until the next chapter. It will be assumed that the mere interaction of determinant components is not what Whitehead is after in his doctrine of freedom, and that such an interaction can not in any case provide a tolerable doctrine of freedom. The present section is therefore devoted to the question whether the doctrine of 'teleological self-creation,' or the 'final reaction of the self-creative unity of the universe,' taken in a sense compatible with subject-hood, is borne out by the theory of creativity.

There is a striking difference between the doctrine of creativity as it is given its definitive form in *Process and Reality*, and the adumbration of the same doctrine in *Science and the Modern World*. In the latter book creativity is described as "an underlying activity—a substantial activity—expressing itself in the individual embodiments

. . ." [1] This activity is said to be substantial in the sense that the new entity that grows out of it is an 'active substance.' On the other hand all these "substances exhibit themselves as the individualisations or modes of Spinoza's one substance." [2] On the face of it there would appear to be a wide gap between this conception and that of *Process and Reality,* in which, as we shall see, creativity is said to be an analogue of Aristotle's matter. Indeed, the description in *Science and the Modern World* of the underlying activity as 'substantial' would appear good warrant for thinking of it as productive of subjects that, as containing more than their components—as containing, indeed, the whole substantial activity—possess an active power making their concrescences more than a mere inner determination by components.

But I do not think that the difference is really so wide. For one thing, the underlying substantial activity is not so much equivalent to the creativity of *Process and Reality* as it is to this creativity taken together with what is called in *Process and Reality* the primordial nature of God. [3] At least this is true of the following passage, which concerns the underlying activity taken in abstraction from the realizations of extensive actuality.

> Finally, to sum up this train of thought, the underlying activity, as conceived apart from the fact of realisation, has three types of envisagement. These are: first, the envisagement of eternal objects; secondly, the envisagement of possibilities of value in respect to the synthesis of eternal objects; and lastly, the envisagement of the actual matter

1. SMW, 152.
2. SMW, 175.
3. The God of *Process and Reality,* then, includes some functions which were, in *Science and the Modern World,* assigned to the substantial activity. In *Process and Reality* God is principle of concretion and contains, as 'envisaged' in his primordial nature, the realm of relevant possibility; while in *Science and the Modern World* God is only the principle of concretion, and the envisagement is the property of the substantial activity. S. L. Ely gives a clear summary of the differences in *The Religious Availability of Whitehead's God* (Madison: The University of Wisconsin Press, 1942); see his note to p. 18; cf. *ibid.,* pp. 8–14.

of fact which must enter into the total situation which is achievable by the addition of the future (SMW, 149).

And I take it that the reason the activity is substantial does not lie necessarily in its containing, when it manifests itself in a particular mode, an active power over and above the determinate components of that mode. I say "necessarily" because the account so far, while it does not forbid this, does not specify it either, but simply refers the *substantiality* of the activity to the envisagements involved in it. Elsewhere the activity seems characterized wholly by these envisagements. Thus in the following passage Whitehead insists that a complete account must include reference both to the static elements in the metaphysical situation and to a complementary activity. Yet he seems also to hold that the activity has *merely* the character given it by the total envisagement.

> In contrast to the realm of possibility the inclusion of eternal objects within an actual occasion means that in respect to some of their possible relationships there is a togetherness of their individual essences. This realised togetherness is the achievement of an emergent value defined—or, shaped—by the definite eternal relatedness in respect to which the real togetherness is achieved . . . ; the emergent actual occasion is the *superject* of informed value . . . and the synthetic activity which prehends valueless possibility into superjicient informed value is the substantial activity. This substantial activity is that which is omitted in any analysis of the static factors in the metaphysical situation. *The analysed elements of the situation are the attributes of the substantial activity* (SMW, 230–31; italics in the last sentence supplied).

Without attempting to be decisive, because we are dealing here with a form of the doctrine that is not final, we can fairly say that one must take Whitehead seriously when he says of the substantial activity that "it is Spinoza's one infinite substance." [4] There is a difference in that Whitehead insists that this substance is an activity, while

4. SMW, 248.

for Spinoza causation has the character of logical necessity. But in both cases the substance is an ultimate reality,
and individual things are modes of it, and apparently
determined by what its character is. And in Whitehead's
case the character of the substantial activity seems ultimately derivable from what is called in *Process and Reality* the primordial nature of God. But even at this point it
is hard to say conclusively what Whitehead's intentions
are. Notice that in the following passage the character of
the underlying activity appears, despite all that I have
just said, to be conditioned but perhaps not determined
by the envisagements that are its attributes.

> The unity of all actual occasions forbids the analysis of sub-
> stantial activities into independent entities. Each individ-
> ual activity is nothing but the mode in which the general
> activity is individualised by the imposed conditions. The
> envisagement which enters into the synthesis is also a
> character which conditions the synthesising activity (SMW,
> 247–48).

To say that "the general activity is individualised by the
imposed conditions" is to imply that the activity has some
character beyond that which the conditions impose.

There appear, then, to be two alternatives. *a)* The
activity in one of its individualized modes has merely the
character given by its envisagements, as well as the character imposed by its other conditions, namely the character of its already completed individualized modes. *b)*
The activity in one of its individualized modes exhibits a
character that is not derivable either from the character of
the envisagements or from the character of the completed
individualized modes. In both these cases, God's function
as principle of concretion is presupposed as still another
of the conditions upon the individualized mode in question; and in the second case it is assumed that what is
inexplicable by the characters cited is not explicable by
God's function. I submit that the doctrine of *Science and
the Modern World* offers no positive evidence that Whitehead intended alternative (*b*), although it may be one

that is appropriate in dealing with the doctrine of *Process and Reality*.

In *Process and Reality* there is at once the major difference that the notion of a *substantial* activity is repudiated.

> In all philosophic theory there is an ultimate which is actual in virtue of its accidents. It is only then capable of characterization through its accidental embodiments, and apart from these accidents is devoid of actuality. In the philosophy of organism this ultimate is termed 'creativity'; and God is its primordial, non-temporal accident. In monistic philosophies, Spinoza's or absolute idealism, this ultimate is God, who is also equivalently termed 'The Absolute.' In such monistic schemes, the ultimate is illegitimately allowed a final, 'eminent' reality, beyond that ascribed to any of its accidents. In this general position the philosophy of organism seems to approximate more to some strains of Indian, or Chinese, thought, than to western Asiatic, or European thought. One side makes process ultimate; the other side makes fact ultimate (PR, 10–11).

Perhaps, though, the change from the seeming Spinozism of *Science and the Modern World* is not so great as one might think; for there the position we are now considering was anticipated in the sense that Whitehead spoke almost as frequently of the 'substantial *activities*' as of the 'substantial *activity*.' But the present explicit statement of the position suggests a way in which the difficulties already found in the exposition of the earlier book can be avoided. Creativity, expressed as the principle of incompleteness, is not exhausted by whatever static character it acquires from God or from the actual world. In fact the only reason it has a *permanent* character is because God is permanent and the actual world objectively immortal. It is itself, though not actual, a source of constant novelty, and if it has produced God as one of its accidents, it may also produce other accidents not contained in those accidents (including God) already produced. It could therefore be thought of as the source of a self-creation beyond the determination of components, because it would indeed only express the fact that a self-creation beyond the determination of all components is the root fact of reality. The self-creation of God by means of which he is an eternal valuation of eternal objects and the self-creation of each of the myriad actual entities would all of them form accidents of an ultimate only actual by virtue of them.

The question now arises not whether self-creation in this sense is plausible, but whether it affords us any useful conception of the "self" that is said to create itself. It seems reasonable that an entity that creates itself should exhibit a coalescence of active power and order. It should actively master the received conditions that for Whitehead constitute actuality, and its creative activity should in doing this draw upon what is actual in a different sense. If we are told, on the contrary, that what in self-creation does not spring from the actuality of the objectively immortal world springs from nowhere, we may agree that this can not be ruled out, but may also wonder why we should call what thus springs into being a *subject*. On Whitehead's ontological principle actual entities furnish all reasons why things are as they are. But if there is in the superjective complex that thus springs into being an element that simply "happens," then that element seems indistinguishable from chance, when "chance" is taken in some radical sense that means more than simply ignorance on our part of some of the conditions of the happening. It is true that William James has used the word "chance" in a well-known essay to designate the causal efficacy of individual subjects,[5] but the word is there used in a strained sense, in order to point out that in the pluralistic world he envisions no one entity can be thought of wholly as a function of all the others. I take it that the word "chance" there protects the irreducibility of the subject, while what I have labeled "chance" in Whitehead's philosophy can be thought of as reducing what is new in the subject to a superjective "happening."[6]

5. William James, "The Dilemma of Determinism," *The Will to Believe and Other Essays in Popular Philosophy* (New York: Longmans, Green and Co., 1904), pp. 145–83.
6. Whitehead has of course acknowledged a deep debt to James. It is deeper, I think, than is generally realized. The essay cited in the

I shall approach this question by emphasizing a difference between Whitehead's doctrine of creativity and that of Bergson. My point is simply that the *élan vital* as Bergson understands it *does* exhibit an order and an active power that are actual in a sense different from the actuality that Whitehead ascribes to the objectified world and different from the settled character Bergson ascribes to the world of material things that the intellect focuses upon.

First consider Bergson's account of creation, which clearly differs from Whitehead's, since it is *identified* with God rather than held to be merely qualified by a creature-God who is a valuation of eternal objects.

> Now if the same kind of action is going on everywhere, whether it is that which is unmaking itself or whether it is that which is striving to remake itself, I simply express this probable similitude when I speak of a centre from which worlds shoot out like rockets in a fire-works display— provided, however, that I do not present this centre as a *thing*, but as a continuity of shooting out. God thus defined, has nothing of the already made; He is increasing life, action, freedom. Creation, so conceived, is not a mystery; we experience it in ourselves when we act freely.[7]

Now I do not want to suggest that such a conception avoids the difficulties that arise in a doctrine of freedom, but mean only to point out that this "continuity of shooting-out" could be called "actual" in a different sense from the one that Whitehead uses. Whitehead's creativity, though described as an 'ultimate behind all forms,' is also said to be 'conditioned by its creatures' (PR, 30). We have

previous note, for instance, may have influenced Whitehead both in his pluralism and in his views on the "limited" nature of God. I do not mean to suggest that James has avoided in his doctrine of freedom difficulties that Whitehead has fallen into. If James's doctrine were as fully developed on this point as Whitehead's the same sort of difficulty about the reality of the subject's causal efficacy might well appear.

7. Henri Bergson, *Creative Evolution,* tr. Arthur Mitchell (New York: Henry Holt & Co., 1913), p. 248.

now to ask with what character, aside from that given by its achieved efforts, creativity makes a new effort.

The term 'creativity' expresses "that ultimate principle by which the many, which are the universe disjunctively, become the one actual occasion, which is the universe conjunctively" (PR, 31). This formulation is hardly more than the Category of the Ultimate, with which we have already dealt, and therefore states Whitehead's fundamental axiom that "the notion of 'passing on' is more fundamental than that of a private individual fact" (PR, 324). So to describe creativity is to leave open the question whether there is an ontological center, in Bergson's sense, out of which this unrest flows. The further description of creativity as not external to actual entities gives us a sense in which there is a subject in Whitehead's philosophy, but still leaves open the question whether each subject is not the (superjective) result of a radical origination rather than the locus of an actively ordering power.

> It is better to say that the feelings *aim at* their subject than that they *are aimed at* their subject. For the latter mode of expression removes the subject from the scope of the feeling and assigns it to an external agency. . . . An actual entity feels as it does feel in order to be the actual entity which it is. In this way an actual entity satisfies Spinoza's notion of substance: it is *causa sui*. The creativity is not an external agency with its own ulterior purposes. All actual entities share with God this character of self-causation. For this reason every actual entity also shares with God the characteristic of transcending all other actual entities, including God (PR, 339).

It should be emphasized at this stage that creativity could be described as not external to its creatures even when we take it in the sense of "creativity" that Bergson intends. And in such a case there might still be meaning—however questionable the conception might be in other respects—to a subject as described in the quotation above. We should simply be saying that the creative source of a creature's status as subject, is always immanent in some subject (or *aim* of feelings *at* a subject), yet is not exhausted by *any* subject. But, on the other hand, in so far as Whitehead's creativity differs from Bergson's, and is positively characterized only by what has already happened, an actual entity must appear either as a super- ject of an activity having such a static character, or in part such a superject, and in part a superject from nowhere in the sense that was questioned earlier. And although we should then be willing to call what thus appears a 'super- ject,' we might still be wary of applying such terms as 'subject' and 'self-creation.'

The major evidence for an interpretation of White- head's creativity as thus different from Bergson's is the statement that creativity is an analogue of Aristotle's mat- ter.

> 'Creativity' is another rendering of the Aristotelian 'mat- ter,' and of the modern 'neutral stuff.' But it is divested of the notion of passive receptivity, either of 'form,' or of external relations; it is the pure notion of the activity conditioned by the objective immortality of the actual world—a world which is never the same twice, though always with the stable element of divine ordering. Creativ- ity is without a character of its own in exactly the same sense in which the Aristotelian 'matter' is without a charac- ter of its own. . . . But creativity is always found under conditions, and described as conditioned (PR, 46–47).

Now I submit that on Bergson's view, although there is no "thing" at the center of the operations of the universe, there is a "character," or rather a superabundance of char- acter; while on Whitehead's view "creativity is without a character of its own" as is Aristotle's matter.

It would appear, then, that creativity, divorced from the ordering given it by one of its creatures—God—is a "mere" activity. The word 'creativity' merely expresses the fact that some indeterminate creature must always emerge, and that the universe is never complete. It does not designate any active power exercised by the subject as such. The claim that creativity is not external to the new creature helps us not at all towards according that crea- ture a status beyond that of superject. We are left with a superject in part unaccounted for (that is its freedom) and in part accounted for by the character given creativity by God and by past actual entities, who in turn ultimately owe their character to God. This last point is expressed in the function of creatures, including God, as objectively immortal.

> This function of creatures, that they constitute the shifting character of creativity, is here termed the 'objective immortality' of actual entities (PR, 47).

This judgment is reinforced by those remarks on creativity that occur in the context of the distinction between real and general potentiality. These will be discussed in the next two chapters, but their tenor can be briefly suggested here. Creativity, considered in abstraction from God and from the actual entities whose order depends on him, is spoken of as 'boundless, abstract possibility'; [8] and it is said that creativity, in abstraction from God, can produce nothing at all. Now once given content by God's valuation the creativity contains a real potentiality, expressed in terms of relations among the eternal objects. It becomes a kind of activity out of which such and such kind of actual entities *can* emerge, by virtue of the relations within the realm of eternal objects, established first by God's valuation of that realm, and second by the settled character of extensive actual occasions that have finished their concrescence. But there remains the question what in the content decides which of the things that *can* issue from the activity *will* issue from it. That is to say, what is the source of the power exercised in the supposed self-creation that determines what is to issue from the real potentiality that qualifies the creativity?

There seem to be no powers except the "powers" of the eternal objects which, as real potentiality, qualify the creativity. Either the choice among real potentialities must be made by something that is already actual (in Whitehead's sense)—for instance, initial subjective aim —or it must appear to come from nowhere. In the for-

8. PR, 336.

mer case it is hard to see how the realm of real potentiality is the realm of possibility, as it is said to be, since
'possibility' (in Whitehead's View) implies alternatives
that are genuine alternatives. There are difficulties in the
latter case as well. Although it may possibly be consist-
ently maintained in some metaphysical doctrines that a
choice should spring from nowhere, it is a claim that does
not sort well, as we have seen, with the expressions 'subject' and 'self-creation.' If we put this in terms of a slightly
different context and ask just how a self-creation could
modify its initial subjective aim except by way of its
already determinate other feelings, we find that there is no
source in creativity from which the modification could
spring. Thus, either elements from the objective lure must
be admitted into the reality of conceptual feeling because
of the determinate prior conceptual and physical feelings,
or this admission must be a circumstance that "just happens."

The analogy with Aristotle's matter that Whitehead
himself draws is a helpful one, and enables us to say that
creativity expresses the incompletability of the universe
only in the sense that it is insatiable as to the form it
receives in real togetherness. Because Whitehead insists
that he intends creativity not as a bare receptivity but as
an activity, we must, however, think of this insatiability as
an activity. Determination of what is to be absorbed (into
real togetherness) by this insatiable indetermination is
either brought about entirely by the forms or eternal
objects that already have real togetherness in it (including initial subjective aim, as established by God) or comes
about arbitrarily. In the latter case we have the only kind
of self-creation that is supported by Whitehead's doctrine,
and it seems to sort better with an explanation in terms of
the arbitrary appearance of a superject than with an explanation in terms of self-creation by a subject. Self-
creation, if it means anything, seems to mean the arbitrary
appearance of a certain togetherness of eternal objects. In
the former case, there is a radical finalism, since all determinations will eventually be traceable to God.

There is, of course, no doubt that Whitehead intends us to take creativity seriously, and that he does not intend to fall into a radical finalism. So extreme is the claim made for the ultimate character of creativity that all the order in the universe can be thought of as a superject of its ceaseless and neutral activity. If we consider the character of creativity at any given point in time, it is not of course neutral, since it is qualified by God's primordial nature and by all the settled and objectively immortal extensive actual entities proper to that point. But even God (who of course is responsible for part of the order of any extensive actual entity) is said to be an 'accident' or creature of this restless activity. And so, though we may not wish to quarrel with the claim that order springs into being *ex nihilo,* it is hard to attach much meaning to the claim that what is at issue is the *self*-creation of entities that are in *some* sense subjects. *Mutatis mutandis,* one thinks of Sartre's claim, in *The Trancendence of the Ego,*[9] that each instant of conscious life is a creation *ex nihilo* of which *we* (the *Ego*) are not the creators. And as for Sartre it would be odd to think of the Ego as an *entity,* since it is in fact a mask, an illusion of something that abides, that consciousness creates to keep from facing its own perfect, and perfectly empty, freedom; so it is perhaps questionable to think of Whitehead's actualities as deserving that name *entity.*

Creativity and power

In order to make clearer the discussion of power in the chapters that follow, where the relation of the notion of power to the doctrine of eternal objects is developed, two basic senses of power will be briefly summarized at this point.

That which exercises efficient causation in Whitehead's philosophy exhibits power, as we have seen, but the

9. Jean-Paul Sartre, *The Transcendence of the Ego,* tr. Forrest William and Robert Kirkpatrick (New York: Noonday Press, 1957), pp. 98–101.

power so exhibited is not an active power. It is rather the power of that which is an *object,* in Whitehead's special sense: settled, actual, determinate, concrete rather than in concrescence. Its characteristics are therefore given in terms of eternal objects. The root sense of power here is the definiteness given to an actual entity by an eternal object having ingression in it; and this sense is related to the notion of potentiality, or possibility, by calling an eternal object a potential because it is a power that can be exercised in alternative ways. These alternative ways merely refer to the fact that the eternal object in question may have real togetherness in the actual entity with various other eternal objects, so that the whole question of the exercise of power in efficient causation is ultimately referable to the ingression of eternal objects in certain patterns.

Now if we think of Whitehead's self-creation, or self-causation, or final causation, as the exercise of power in another sense, we must think of it, if it is to be genuinely exercised *by* a subject, as an active rather than a static power. The objections brought by way of criticism of the doctrine of creativity revealed that creativity provided no source for such a power. Restating the conclusions of the previous section in terms of power, we can say that the self-causation, or self-creation, of an actual entity can be understood as the incorporation in it of a selection of static powers (eternal objects), which thus acquire real togetherness. This process in turn can be understood in two ways. *a)* The incorporation takes place entirely by way of the determination of static powers already incorporated in the actual entity. *b)* The incorporation takes place in part by way of already incorporated static powers, and in part simply "happens" as an accident of creativity. The first way gives us a radical finalism centered upon God, although qualified by the sense in which he is *also* an accident of creativity; the second gives us the origination *ex nihilo* in the sense, inhospitable to the idea 'subject,' discussed at the close of the previous section.

The metaphorical character of certain of the ideas in

terms of which Whitehead's doctrine of freedom is developed does much to obscure this conclusion. Most promi-
nent are such notions as 'lure' and 'persuasion,' which
have the aspect of honorific metaphors in a context where
freedom is a desirable characteristic. There must always
be something that is to be persuaded, or something that is
to be lured, if these words are to have any meaning.
Indeed the terms presuppose that there is a kind of recal-
citrance of something or other as over against the efforts
of God. This must appear as some kind of power, and yet,
if our analysis is tolerably accurate, it would seem that, if
anything is lured or persuaded, it is a pure indetermination, or prime matter.

Subject, superject, mode, internal and external relations

It has been noticed at more than one point that Whitehead prefers the term 'superject' to the term 'subject,' and
that where he uses the latter term he intends it to stand
for 'subject-superject.' We must now relate these facts in a
more conclusive way to the present criticism of creativity.

There is at least one sense of 'subject' necessary to the
doctrine of freedom Whitehead seeks to sustain, and that
is the sense in which the concrescence of an actual entity
is understood as more than a reaction one upon another of
determinate components. For feelings to be the feelings of
a free subject the component feelings must have a unity
which does not appear as a mere togetherness of determinate feelings dominated by one determinate feeling (the
subjective aim). Of course, if all that one requires of the
notion 'subject' is that it exist in itself and that other
things appear as modes of it, then the 'substantial activity'
of *Science and the Modern World,* considered as endowed
with a fixed character by God, could perhaps provide it,
although with monistic consequences. But this subject
would then have the eminent reality forbidden by Whitehead; and even if it were an acceptable subject on these
grounds, it would still not be the kind of individual sub-

ject necessary for Whitehead's doctrine of freedom. Whitehead's frank use of the term 'mode' in *Science and the Modern World* parallels his use of the term 'superject,' and suggests a preference for this way of looking at reality that goes somewhat incongruously with the doctrine of freedom. It is an example of the frequent use in his philosophy of terms that seem to make an actual entity appear as entirely a resultant, rather than as itself exercising a causation.

The fact that it seems possible to think of an actual entity as consisting entirely of internal relations is a case in point. I would here define internal relations,[10] with Whitehead, as a relation contributing to the determinateness of an actual entity, and whose absence would make a difference to the real internal constitution of that entity. This at once makes our discussion of internal relations parallel to the discussion of determinate components throughout the present chapter. It would seem fair to say that the active power here deemed necessary to a proper doctrine of a free subject would be a power having external relations as well. The field of our discussion must be closely circumscribed at this point. Here no more is meant by this contention than that the power must be capable of relations that do not determine it as internal relations, in the sense just explained, would determine it. Thus, in this sense of external relations, an entity described in terms of feeling would be externally related to each of several elements that it *might* feel, where it need not feel any particular one of them. In this sense possible internal relations are, *qua* possible, external relations. But note that in an actual entity already internally related to certain felt elements, there can be no such external relations unless there is present in the entity an active power over and above the internal relations in question. If such a power is not present, any external relations (in our sense) would be specious, for later internal relations would be determined by present ones, or, on the alternative in-

10. In one sense of relation. See the discussion of relations in chapter 2, section A1.

terpretation, which preserves creativity but not the subject, would merely "happen."

It may well be that our demand for external relations is merely a requirement of substantiality, for that which consists wholly of internal relations seems to be merely a mode in a complex more substantial than itself. It is at any rate suggested here that an actual entity possessing freedom under conditions must *a)* be internally related to those conditions; *b)* become successively related internally to other elements, i.e. the entity must develop; *c)* exhibit an active power related externally to elements that are relevant to its future but may or may not enter into it.

Recapitulation of the argument of chapters 3 and 4

In this and the previous chapter, in the course of an exposition of 'self-causation,' 'subjective aim,' and 'creativity,' two main criticisms were brought against Whitehead's theory of freedom. Both concerned the reality, or at any rate the autonomy, of the modifications subjective aim was said to undergo. But the first of the objections was offered only tentatively, and the burden of the argument was allowed to rest on the second objection.

The first objection had to do with the relation of the epochal theory of time to the so-called modification of subjective aim in the course of the concrescence. By this theory the mental pole—and therefore subjective aim—is said to be indivisible, but the physical pole is divisible, and reflects this divisibility back into the coordinate division of the actual entity, in which coordinate division physical time appears. It was suggested that the exemption of the mental pole from divisibility might make it necessary to regard the so-called development of subjective aim as merely an illusion arising from looking at it from the point of view of the divisibility of the physical pole. On these grounds alone the charge of radical finalism might be brought, and one might say that the whole development observable in the physical pole merely reflected the need of a successiveness to unfold the pattern of feelings dictated by the mental pole.

The second objection arose only when the first was waived on the grounds that, when Whitehead describes the mental pole as an indivisible unity and still insists on the reality of the development of subjective aim, his meaning is not entirely clear. In this second and more decisive objection, the reality of the modification of subjective aim was accepted, but it was urged that this modification might be given two interpretations. It might appear either as the effect of determinate components one upon the other, or as a modification more properly called a free one. The first interpretation was held—quite generally, and without any detailed investigation—to fit all of Whitehead's theory except the doctrine of freedom, and attention was then concentrated on an attempt to show that the second interpretation would not hold. Here the doctrine of creativity was examined, and it was pointed out that creativity did not appear to be the source of any (active) power to bring about the modification of the subjective aim, so that this modification must seem to come about *ex nihilo*, or to result from the character of determinate components. No objection was made to creativity as productive of novelty *ex nihilo* (though objections could be made). It was held, however, that this doctrine was inconsistent with the idea of an actual entity considered as a *self*-creative *subject*.

5

THE CRITICISM:

Eternal objects and *power*

Eternal objects as potentials: the source of power

WHITEHEAD PREFERS to avoid the term 'universals' in favor of the term 'eternal objects,' because the usual opposition between universal and particular neglects the sense in which "every so-called 'universal' is particular in the sense of being just what it is, diverse from everything else," and the sense in which every " 'particular' is universal in entering into the constitutions of other actual entities" (PR, 76). Other reasons for preferring the term 'eternal object' are given as follows.

> The term 'Platonic form' has here been used as the briefest way of indicating the entities in question. But . . . the entities in question are not necessarily restricted to those which he would recognize as 'forms.' Also the term 'idea' has a subjective suggestion in modern philosophy, which is very misleading for my present purposes; and in any case it has been used in many senses and has become ambiguous. The term 'essence,' as used by the Critical Realists, also suggests their use of it, which diverges from what I intend. Accordingly, by way of employing a term devoid of misleading suggestions, I use the phrase 'eternal object'. . . . Any entity whose conceptual recognition does not involve a necessary reference to any definite actual entities of the temporal world is called an 'eternal object' (PR, 69–70).

The mention of conceptual recognition in the last sentence is a reminder of Whitehead's earlier epistemological writings. But questions of the origin and earlier forms of the doctrine do not belong so much to the present concern as does the place the doctrine has in his speculative metaphysics. Accordingly attention will be directed to the description of eternal objects as 'Pure Potentials for the Specific Determination of Fact,' or 'Forms of Definiteness' (PR, 76), the latter description being elsewhere elaborated as 'potentialities of definiteness for any actual existence' (PR, 63). The following passage summarizes this line of thought.

> If the term 'eternal objects' is disliked, the term 'potentials' would be suitable. The eternal objects are the pure potentials of the universe; and the actual entities differ from each other in their realization of potentials (PR, 226).

The root sense of potentiality is indeterminateness, but when it is said that an eternal object is that which is indeterminate, it is not meant that the eternal object in itself lacks definiteness, but rather that the eternal object is indeterminate as to its mode of ingression in any actual entity. It is the notion of the 'individual essence' of an eternal object that forbids our thinking of it as indefinite in itself; this notion will be developed later, but it should be kept in mind in connection with a passage like the following.

> An eternal object in abstraction from any one particular actual entity is a potentiality for ingression into actual entities. In its ingression into any one actual entity, either as relevant or as irrelevant, it retains its potentiality of indefinite diversity of modes of ingression, a potential indetermination rendered determinate in this instance. The definite ingression into a particular actual entity is not to be conceived as the sheer evocation of that eternal object from 'not-being' into 'being'; it is the evocation of determination out of indetermination. Potentiality becomes reality; and yet retains its message of alternatives which the actual entity has avoided (PR, 226).

Here there is no mention of the definiteness of eternal objects; but it must be remembered that they are always "things which constitute the potentialities of definiteness for any actual existence" (PR, 63), and that they can only bring definiteness if they are in themselves definite. When it is said that potentiality is an "indetermination, rendered determinate in the real concrescence" (PR, 34) it is only meant that definite entities are indeterminate as to how they will contribute their definiteness. Indeed this indetermination of potentiality makes sense only as a corollary of an actuality in which the definiteness of the eternal objects is actually exercised. The whole status of eternal objects is that of entities indeterminate as to their ingression in actuality, but in themselves determinate yet inefficient.

It is worth noticing at this point that Whitehead's use of the term 'potentiality' and its correlate 'actuality' is in general different from Aristotle's, although there are some similarities. The realm of actuality for Whitehead is defined by the completed or objectified actual entities at any given point, and their completeness in turn is defined by a permanent qualification of the realm of eternal objects. Actuality thus includes God, who is eternally complete, together with all the finite actual entities up to the point in process that is in question. Of course if Whitehead's system is in fact a radical finalism centered on God, all actuality would be dependent upon God's actuality as it is in the case of Aristotle. Actuality in this sense determines the range of what *can* happen in the future although it does not determine precisely what *will* happen. In this sense actuality determines what real potentiality is at any given point. This is the 'power' of actuality and real potentiality is therefore process qualified by the power of what is already actual. In so far as the Aristotelian conception of potentiality (or matter) is a relative one, the conceptions are thus similar. But the Aristotelian conception of *pure* potentiality is that of *prime* matter, and this corresponds to Whitehead's conception of creativity in abstraction from what qualifies it (in abstraction from what is really potential in it in Whitehead's sense), rather than to his view of general potentiality. The latter is defined by what eternal objects *independently of their qualification by actual entities* dictate. In sum, the term *potentiality* as Whitehead uses it always includes some reference to the power exercised by forms or eternal objects, and this is surely not always the case in Aristotle.

The seventh of the "Categories of Explanation" expresses both the definiteness of eternal objects and the fact that their whole status is to be potentials, indeterminate as regards inclusion in actuality.

vii] That an eternal object can be described only in terms of its potentiality for 'ingression' into the becoming of actual entities; and that its analysis only discloses other eternal objects. It is a pure potential. The term 'ingression' refers to the particular mode in which the potentiality of an eternal object is realized in a particular actual entity, contributing to the definiteness of that actual entity (PR, 34).

More will be said about these two sides of an eternal object in the later discussion of individual essence, and in the discussion of the relations into which eternal objects can enter. Here the notion 'mode of ingression' is important for a deeper understanding of the nature of potentiality. The problem is best approached by anticipating for a moment our discussion of the distinction between general (or boundless and abstract) potentiality, and real potentiality. In defining the former Whitehead always notices that it is what potentiality would be if it were abstracted from the satisfactions of all actual entities, including God; and frequently he refers to it as a *disjunction*.

The two sets [of temporal and eternal things] are mediated by a thing which combines the actuality of what is temporal with the timelessness of what is potential. This final entity is the divine element in the world, *by which the barren inefficient disjunction of abstract potentialities* obtains primordially the efficient conjunction of ideal realization. This ideal realization of potentialities in a primordial actual entity constitutes the metaphysical stability whereby the actual process exemplifies general principles of metaphysics, and attains the ends proper to specific types of emergent order. By reason of the actuality of this primordial valuation of pure potentials, each eternal object has a definite, effective relevance to each concrescent process. *Apart from such ordering, there would be a complete disjunction of eternal objects unrealized in the temporal world* (PR, 63–64; italics supplied).

It is the notion of disjunction that I wish to seize upon; for it suggests that by a 'mode of ingression' of an eternal object Whitehead means merely the togetherness, or efficient conjunction,[1] of a set of eternal objects. And this in turn suggests that at the root of the term 'potential' as applied to eternal objects is the mere manyness or the disjunction of them: when we say that an eternal object is a potential (and as such indeterminate) we must mean simply that there are other eternal objects, with some of which it must when actual be in efficient conjunction. To conceive of eternal objects as potentials because they form a disjunction in the absence of an 'agency of comparison' is not to speak of them as in themselves indefinite: that which is indeterminate in them is the fact of their disjunction.

The relations between the notions 'power' and 'possibility' may be discussed conveniently at this point. Of the later it need only be said that Whitehead seems to use it interchangeably with 'potentiality.' Thus 'boundless, abstract possibility' is used interchangeably with 'general potentiality';[2] and elsewhere[3] the same practice is followed, although 'potentiality' appears to be the commoner term. As we have seen, 'power' bears upon 'potentiality' in a more complicated way. Discarding Whitehead's relation to Locke in this matter, one can say that the notion 'power' is bound up with the notion 'objectification,' with which I have already dealt.[4] This reveals that the term

1. This notion awaits further definition, but the earlier discussion of 'contrasts' (see chapter 2, section CIII) has already anticipated some of the main points.

2. PR, 336.

3. E.g., PR, 46, 21.

4. Chapter 2, section B.

finds its explicit use chiefly in a context of actual entities rather than of eternal objects. The following passage should be clear enough in its bearing on our present problems to stand quotation without the lengthy excerpt from Locke that precedes it.

> In this important passage, Locke enunciates the main doctrines of the philosophy of organism, namely . . . the relational character of eternal objects, whereby they constitute the forms of the objectifications of actual entities for each other; . . . the notion of 'power' as making a principle ingredient in that of actual entity (substance). In this latter notion, Locke adumbrates both the ontological principle, and also the principle that the 'power' of one actual entity on the other is simply how the former is objectified in the constitution of the other. Thus the problem of perception and the problem of power are one and the same, at least so far as perception is reduced to mere prehension of actual entities (PR, 91).

I shall first discuss the bearing of the notion of power upon that of potentiality, attending only to the relation of these conceptions to actual entities, and shall then broaden the discussion in a way hinted at in the above passage, where "the relational character of eternal objects, whereby they constitute the forms of the objectification of actual entities for each other," is noticed.

If what is objectified exerts power, then what is an object but is not yet objectified in a given entity has a potentiality for exerting power. Here 'potentiality' means that the object *could* be objectified in many ways. There is the same contrast here as that between an eternal object considered merely as a potentiality and an eternal object considered as a *potentiality of definiteness*. The power that an objectified *actual entity* exerts is analogous to the definiteness supplied by an *eternal object* that has ingression in a certain actual entity. And both the objectified actual entity and the ingressing eternal object retain the potentiality of performing different functions in different entities.

The interpretation of 'object' here adopted depends on passages like the following.

The word 'object' thus means an entity which is a potentiality for being a component in feeling; and the word
'subject' means the entity constituted by the process of
feeling, and including this process. The feeler is the unity
emergent from its own feelings; and feelings are the details of the process intermediary between this unity and its
many data. The data are the potentials for feelings; that is
to say, they are objects. The process is the elimination of
indeterminateness of feeling from the unity of one subjective experience (PR, 136).

It will at once be noticed that the word 'objects' in the
above can apply either to eternal objects or to actual
entities. This rather supports my point than otherwise, for
it was my intention to draw a parallel between the perfectly definite character of an eternal object, which can
yet ingress in many ways, and the perfectly definite and
settled character of an actual entity (taken as object),
which can yet enter into another actual entity in many
ways. When the eternal object ingresses in a definite
mode, it contributes just that definiteness; when an actual
entity is objectified in a certain way, it exercises just that
power. In both cases the notion of potentiality is the
notion of power or definiteness indeterminate as to the
mode in which it is to contribute. And here the ideas of
power and of definiteness seem identical, for when an
eternal object is conceptually felt, we can speak of it on
the above quotation either as contributing definiteness or
as exercising power.

It is not far from considering an actual entity as playing a role similar to that of an eternal object, to the
question whether that role of the actual entity is not made
possible by its being a togetherness of eternal objects. And
in support of this, the reader will recall that it was earlier
brought out that eternal objects have a "relational character, whereby they constitute the forms of the objectifications of actual entities for each other" (PR, 91). The point
has long since been made that physical feelings, no less
than conceptual feelings, are by way of eternal objects,[5]

5. Chapter 2, section AII.

and additional supporting passages are not wanting. One leaps easily to the conclusion that all power and potentiality are reducible ultimately to eternal objects. This conclusion is first of all a tentative one; and in the second place it rests on the assumption, made in our earlier discussion of creativity, that there is no other sense of power in Whitehead's metaphysics. We are also taking in an unanalyzed fashion such a notion as the 'togetherness' of eternal objects; and are assuming that, because an actual entity can be so described, its substantiality (or status as a being) is made derivative from eternal objects, these latter being taken as ontologically more "ultimate." These assumptions will require defense in the next chapter.

Real and general potentiality; how real potentiality is produced

It is the purpose of the present section   A] to outline the differences between real and general potentiality;   B] to examine the sense in which actual entities, both actual occasions and God, are alleged to contribute by their 'agency' to real potentiality; and then,   C] to raise again the question of the source of the power that would have to be exercised in this agency.

A] It has already been noticed that eternal objects, in abstraction from the actual entities of the world, are held to constitute a "barren inefficient disjunction of abstract potentialities" (PR, 64). The idea of indeterminateness in the notion of potentiality was held to refer most precisely to that inefficient disjunction, eternal objects being perfectly definite in their individual essences. The use of the term 'inefficient' does no more than recognize that 'potentiality' requires its correlate 'actuality,' for an inefficient disjunction is inefficient only as over against the efficient togetherness of eternal objects (the 'flux of forms') in the actuality of a real concrescence. Whitehead's own distinction between real and general potentiality may now be introduced.

Thus we have always to consider two meanings of potentiality: *a*) the 'general' potentiality, which is the bundle of possibilities, mutually consistent or alternative, provided by the multiplicity of eternal objects, and *b*) the 'real' potentiality, which is conditioned by the data provided by the actual world. General potentiality is absolute, and real potentiality is relative to some actual entity taken as a standpoint whereby the actual world is defined. . . . The actual world must always mean the community of all actual entities, including the primordial actual entity called 'God' and the temporal actual entities (PR, 101–2).

To return to disjunction as the root sense of potentiality: a disjunction that is not completely inefficient is one that is somehow qualified. Now Whitehead holds that only an actuality, i.e. some actual entity, can really bring about such qualification. Our task at this point is to determine just how actual entities bring about this qualification, with the view to determining eventually whether any genuine agency is involved.

B] Whitehead refers to as 'relevance' what is here termed a qualified disjunction of eternal objects, or a qualified potentiality. "Effective relevance," he says, "requires agency of comparison, and agency belongs exclusively to actual occasions." The whole passage may be useful, because it outlines the root sense in which actuality is said to qualify general potentiality to produce real potentiality.

> The primordial created fact is the unconditioned conceptual valuation of the entire multiplicity of eternal objects. This is the 'primordial nature' of God. By reason of this complete valuation, the objectification of God in each derivative actual entity results in a graduation of the relevance of eternal objects to the concrescent phases of that derivative occasion. There will be additional ground of relevance for select eternal objects by reason of their ingression into derivative actual entities belonging to the actual world of the concrescent occasion in question. But whether or no this be the case, there is always the definite relevance derived from God. Apart from God, eternal objects unrealized in the actual world would be relatively non-

existent for the concrescence in question. For effective relevance requires agency of comparison, and agency belongs exclusively to actual occasions (PR, 46).

On the basis of this account, real potentiality for any given actual entity consists in the totality of eternal objects as these are qualified, or made relevant, by the objectification in the actual entity of God and of other actual entities. The objectification of God in the actual entity is equivalent to its having an initial subjective aim. The objectification in it of other actual entities as well is described as the "additional ground of relevance for select eternal objects by reason of their ingression into derivative actual entities belonging to the actual world of the concrescent occasion in question." The earlier discussion of the word 'object' as used in Whitehead revealed that it meant an "entity which is a potentiality for being a component in a feeling"—that is to say, something with the kind of definiteness that makes it a datum for feeling yet indeterminate as to just how it shall be felt. Here God might be a datum for feeling in many ways, and so might the actual world of the concrescence in question. But they must be felt in *some* way, and this sets a limit upon the indeterminateness of eternal objects as to their ingression into the actual entity in question. Thus real potentiality represents the condition put upon one kind of objects, or data for feeling, namely eternal objects, by the determinate way in which another kind of objects, namely actual entities, are in fact felt. Such an interpretation should clarify a passage like the following.

> This 'given' world provides determinate data in the form of those objectifications of themselves which the characters of its actual entities can provide. This is a limitation laid upon the general potentiality provided by eternal objects, considered merely in respect to the generality of their natures. Thus, relatively to any actual entity, there is a 'given' world of settled actual entities and a 'real' potentiality, which is the datum for creativeness beyond that standpoint. This datum which is the primary phase in the process constituting an actual entity, is nothing else than

the actual world itself in its character of a possibility of
being felt (PR, 101).

The closing sentence makes it clear that the real potentiality, provided by the fact that a given world is objectified
in a certain way, is in one sense the realm of eternal
objects qualified by that objectification, and in another
sense that objectified world qualified by the relevance to it
of the realm of eternal objects. This is the "actual world
itself in its character of being felt."

So far the discussion of the distinction between general and real potentiality has seen the latter emerging as
the result of the agency of actual entities, but it has
concentrated not on the alleged internal self-creative
character of this agency, but on its *effects*. That is to say
we have concentrated on the 'power' of actual entities in
their existence *objectivé*—on their existence as "definite,
determinate, settled fact, stubborn and with unavoidable
consequences" (PR, 336). And we have found that it is by
this aspect that they produce real potentiality. In this
sense of power an actual entity has the kind of definiteness an eternal object has; and, like the eternal object, it is
indeterminate as to how it is to contribute to some entity
that will prehend it. Before a new actuality emerges from
a situation riddled with ambiguity, the ambiguity is already conditioned by the existence *objectivé* (as a satisfaction, or datum for feeling) of actual entities already in
existence, and to which the new actuality must in some
sense conform.

> This objective intervention of other entities constitutes the
> creative character which conditions the concrescence in
> question. The satisfaction of each actual entity is an ele-
> ment in the givenness of the universe: it limits boundless,
> abstract possibility into the particular real potentiality from
> which each novel concrescence originates. The 'boundless,
> abstract possibility' means the creativity considered solely
> in reference to the possibilities of the intervention of
> eternal objects, and in abstraction from the objective inter-
> vention of actual entities belonging to any definite actual

world, including God among the entities abstracted from
(PR, 336–37).

The way in which the new actual entity does in fact
conform at the outset—its initial subjective aim, or its
settled viewpoint—is the way in which actual entities are
in fact objectified in the new entity. One may also say that
it is the way in which their power makes itself felt. This
limits real potentiality in a more particular way.

The account thus far may be summarized by saying
that general potentiality is an indeterminateness on the
part of eternal objects as to their mode of ingression in
actual entities, the eternal objects being in themselves
perfectly definite and determinate; while real potentiality
is this indeterminateness qualified by the power possessed
by actual entities. The difference is that between pure
indetermination and conditioned indetermination.[6] But
the conditioning is here brought about by powers that
have that status because they are constituted by a togetherness of other powers—the eternal objects. Here the term
'powers' refers to the *definiteness* of either an eternal
object or an actual entity, which definiteness is referred to
as 'potentiality' if it is indeterminate as to its exercise.
Thus both 'general potentiality' and 'real potentiality' include both the notion of definiteness and that of indetermination, but the indetermination factor in the former is
pure, which in the latter it is conditioned. 'General potentiality,' 'real potentiality,' and 'objective lure' all contain,
as has been said, the notion of indetermination, and it
should be reiterated here, in anticipation of later developments, that in each case the indetermination refers to a
disjunction of eternal objects. But in the case of real
potentiality the disjunction of eternal objects is conditioned,[7] and the indetermination is therefore a conditioned indetermination.

The internal character of the agencies whose effects
are powers qualifying real potentiality is said to be feel-

6. PR, 34.
7. The meaning of this is given in the next chapter.

ing. All inclusion in actuality is an inclusion in feeling, just as all real potentiality represents data for feeling. This is true for the extensive actual entities with which we dealt at length in chapter 2. It is no less true for God, who is the actual entity corresponding to the requirement of the ontological principle that potentiality must, like everything else, be somewhere.

> Everything must be somewhere; and here 'somewhere' means 'some actual entity.' Accordingly the general potentiality of the universe must be somewhere; since it retains its proximate relevance to actual entities for which it is unrealized. This 'proximate relevance' reappears in subsequent concrescence as final causation regulative of the emergence of novelty. This 'somewhere' is the nontemporal actual entity. Thus 'proximate relevance' means 'relevance as in the primordial mind of God' (PR, 73).

Here the use of the word 'general' as modifying 'potentiality' seems an inadvertence on Whitehead's part, for surely he is here talking of real potentiality (or that part of it for which God's agency is responsible) rather than of general potentiality, as the idea of 'relevance' assures us. In the course of expanding the above remarks Whitehead goes on to say that "subsistence" means "how eternal objects can be components of the primordial nature of God." This question of subsistence will reappear later, but here it is pertinent that God's function, by which the ideal component of real potentiality is somewhere, and by which eternal objects subsist, is a functioning analogous to what we have called feeling (or prehension) in the case of extensive actual entities. In God's case the functioning is however referred to as a 'valuation' or an 'envisagement.'[8] This internal character of God's agency as well as that of extensive actual entities is frequently referred to as a 'decision' among 'givenness.'

> For rationalistic thought, the notion of 'givenness' carries with it a reference beyond the mere data in question. It refers to a 'decision' whereby what is 'given' is separated

8. PR, 69, 70.

off from what for that occasion is 'not given.' This element of 'givenness' in things implies some activity procuring limitation. . . . The ontological principle declares that every decision is referable to one or more actual entities. . . . But 'decision' cannot be construed as a casual adjunct of an actual entity. It constitutes the very meaning of actuality. An actual entity arises from decisions *for* it, and by its very existence provides decisions *for* other actual entities which supersede it. . . . 'Actuality' is the decision amid 'potentiality.' It represents stubborn fact which cannot be evaded. The real internal constitution of an actual entity progressively constitutes a decision conditioning the creativity which transcends that actuality (PR, 68–69).

This decision describes how feeling, or in the case of God, envisagement, constitutes the entity in question as a determinate power, indeterminate as to how it is to be felt. In this guise of determinate power the entity (whether God or an actual occasion) qualifies real potentiality. Indeed, in the explicit doctrine, decision is fairly described as that by which real potentiality grows.

c] If a finished actual entity has qualified real potentiality by virtue of the definiteness it has as a real togetherness of eternal objects; if it exercises, that is, in its finished state a static power analogous to the static power of eternal objects; it would seem that we must attribute to it some prior *active* power in its process of self-causation. At least it would seem that we must do this if we are to attribute the power exercised *after* it has completed its course to that *actual entity* that was once in process, and of which we persist in using such terminology as 'exercise of decision' and 'agency of comparison.' The discussion of creativity in the preceding chapter [9] suggests that Whitehead's doctrine will not support this conception of active power, at least not if we suppose that active power is power exercised by a subject. There the point was made that actual entities must be thought of as primarily superjective. They are, that is, thrown up either by *a)* a creativity character-

9. See chapter 4, pp. 37–42.

ized only by the prior real togetherness of eternal objects or by *b)* a creativity characterized positively only as in *(a)* but having the "capacity" to contribute to its creatures from a blank indetermination as well as from that positive character. If the characters such superjective actual entities have in their completed state are given in terms of eternal objects that are in real togetherness, it is possible to suggest that these supposedly concrete actual entities are epiphenomenal nodes on a 'flux of forms' more ultimate than they. Indeed, if no agency or active power brings about real togetherness, then the togetherness does seem ultimate, and the actual entity truly a superject of that togetherness.

It will be noted that in case *(a)* above the creativity is eventually characterized by the static power of the primordial nature of God. Since creativity would then owe all its character to the real togetherness of eternal objects that is the primordial nature of God, we should in fact have a radical finalism. Or we should have one if we neglected the claim that God too is an accident of creativity. In case *(b)* the emergence of new togetherness is so arbitrary as to be indistinguishable from chance. It appears that on the absence of an active power to give agency in the sense of a subject, the sense in which eternal objects "exist" is made the basis for the sense in which actual entities exist. This is the basis for our use of the term "Platonism" in the next chapter. Alternatively we must get our sense of "exist" from the sense in which an activity as blank as prime matter—or, as we have said, a blank insatiability for forms—exists.

But in the present chapter and in the next our intent is not so much to elaborate the thesis of chapters 3 and 4 as to show that the ramifications of the doctrine of eternal objects are such as to be consistent with that thesis. The argument begun in this chapter and completed in the concluding chapter purports, then, to show that the theory of feeling, and the theory of the qualification of real potentiality by actual entities, is explainable without remainder in terms of the togetherness—of a certain sort—of eternal objects. It is maintained that the character of eternal objects is such as to enable them, alone among all the elements of Whitehead's universe, to exist in and through themselves while other types of existence are in some sense derivative from theirs. They thus display at least some of the marks traditionally associated with substantiality—or, if one prefers to avoid the many unfortunate overtones of that rendering of the term *"ousia,"* traditionally associated with the status of an *entity.* The completion of our argument requires, therefore, an investigation of the sort of relations that can exist between eternal objects, between actual entities, and between these two types of entities.

6

THE CRITICISM:

The Platonism of Whitehead

Preliminary definitions

IN CALLING Whitehead a Platonist I intend to make only a relatively simple point. It is that despite all his insistence on the principle of coherence, which holds that none of the conceptions of a philosophy is fully meaningful without its relations to all the others, he does in fact accord eternal objects—his version of Platonic Forms—more of the traditional marks of substantiality than he does other ingredients of his system. In particular, I shall urge that the ontological principle, which Whitehead has conveniently summed up for us in the formula "no actual entity, then no reason" (PR, 28), plays a less important role in his philosophy than his explicit references to it would lead us to believe.[1] If we take the references to the ontological principle as indicating a roughly Aristotelian intent on Whitehead's part, my point can be restated in fairly modest terms. It is simply that the chief *emphasis* in Whitehead's system appears after analysis to lie upon the role of eternal objects, and that the Aristotelian theme of the ontological principle is a less important one. I am using the expressions "Platonic" and "Aristotelian" in a rough and ready way at this point. What I intend by the expression "the Platonism of Whitehead" will become clear in the course of the chapter.

---

1. That principle might itself be cited as a violation of the principle of coherence, in that it would *seem* to give actual entities a thoroughly privileged status.

It may be helpful if I insist once again it is plain that it is Whitehead's *intent* to avoid either a "Platonic" or an "Aristotelian" emphasis. The following quotation makes his position quite clear, and even exhibits the word "Platonic" in a sense suitable to that intent.

> The true philosophic question is, How can concrete fact exhibit entities abstract from itself and yet participated in by its own nature?
>
> In other words, philosophy is explanatory of abstraction, and not of concreteness. It is by reason of their instinctive grasp of this ultimate truth that, in spite of much association with arbitrary fancifulness and atavistic mysticism, types of Platonic philosophy retain their abiding appeal; they seek the forms in the facts. Each fact is more than its forms, and each form 'participates' throughout the world of facts. The definiteness of fact is due to its forms; but the individual fact is a creature, and creativity is the ultimate behind all forms, inexplicable by forms, and conditioned by its creatures (PR, 30).

The trouble is, at least on the interpretation upon which we are about to embark, that Whitehead's theory of eternal object fails to bear out this statement of principle.

It is in this spirit that I should have to answer those writers who have maintained that in Whitehead's doctrine actual entities and eternal objects have a coeval status. William A. Christian, in his illuminating discussion of eternal objects in *An Interpretation of Whitehead's Metaphysics*,[2] stresses Whitehead's wish to avoid ascribing to eternal objects a reality totally independent of the actual entities in which they ingress, and also to avoid conceiving of actual entities as understandable without reference to the coeval ontological status of eternal objects. Christian holds not only that it is Whitehead's wish to avoid

2. William A. Christian, *An Interpretation of Whitehead's Metaphysics* (New Haven: Yale University Press, 1959). Part Two, consisting of Chapters 10–14, is devoted to a detailed discussion of the doctrine of eternal objects, including its antecedents in Whitehead's earlier philosophy. In many important respects my thesis about eternal objects is in agreement with Christian's; the points of difference are made clear enough in chapter 6.

both of these extremes, but also, I take it, that he is successful in doing so.[3]

Ivor Leclerc in his essay "Form and Actuality" [4] addresses himself very directly to the claim that Whitehead's doctrine successfully maintains this coeval status. The essay is a valuable one, and clarifies the explicit doctrine on many important points by means of accurate comparisons with the view of Aristotle on form and actuality. He uses the many similarities with Aristotle's doctrine to point up Whitehead's explicit rejection of Platonism, but also points to a fundamental difference between Aristotle and Whitehead. The following passage summarizes one of the chief lines of argument.

> Form cannot, for Whitehead, be supreme, the one metaphysical ultimate, for precisely the reason that it can be that for Aristotle. This reason is that Aristotle identifies act and form, whereas Whitehead rejects that particular identification. In other words, whereas Aristotle ascribes act to form, Whitehead holds that form as such cannot act. Whitehead thus maintains that both poles are requisite if we are to have an adequate metaphysics.
>
> Further, Whitehead holds, both poles are integrally necessary to each other. Our examination of what this entails, however, has shown that form is identified with actuality. It is evident that we have to be careful as to how exactly this 'identification' is to be understood.
>
> In the first place, it does not involve an *equating* of the one with the other. On the contrary, we must here clearly bear in mind that it is the essential and distinctive Whiteheadian doctrine that creativity (act, activity as such) is the 'category of the ultimate.' This means that being, existence, is ultimately grounded in creativity, in 'act.' The relevance of this to form is crucial. It means that form, as such, cannot *be;* the being of form is the enacting of form. And this enacting is not due to form; form 'is enacted'—form does not enact itself.[5]

3. *Ibid.,* pp. 196–200, 277–79, and *passim* Part II.
4. *The Relevance of Whitehead,* ed. Ivor Leclerc (London: George Allen & Unwin; New York: The Macmillan Company, 1961), pp. 169–89.
5. *Ibid.,* pp. 187–88.

The passage perhaps stresses the role form plays in actuality at the expense of its status as potentiality or possibility. Mr. Leclerc does, however, take account of this elsewhere in his essay, and in a way perfectly congruent with his claim here that for Whitehead form is actuality by being "enacted." My own interpretation of what Whitehead's account of creativity and power comes to is obviously at odds with Leclerc's views on the activity of actual entities, but with his and with Christian's account of Whitehead's *wish* to make actual entities and eternal objects coeval I have no quarrel. Leclerc is also right in citing Whitehead's *Modes of Thought* and his final lecture, the Ingersoll lecture on "Immortality," as evidence that he maintained that position to the end. And all this is supported by the additional evidence of Whitehead's 1936 letter to Charles Hartshorne,[6] which leaves no doubt that Whitehead intended to give eternal objects and actual entities a coeval status. The following passage from that letter is decisive enough.

> The points to notice are i] that 'Et. Obj.' are the carriers of potentiality into realization;
> and   ii] that they thereby carry mentality into matter of fact;
> and   iii] that no eternal object in any finite realization can exhibit the full potentialities of its nature. It has an individual essence—whereby it is the same eternal object on diverse occasions, and it has a relational essence whereby it has an infinitude of modes of entry into realization. But realization introduces finitude (in Spinoza's sense), with the extension of the infinitude of incompatibles in the relational essence.
> iv] The relational essence of each 'Etern. Obj.' involves its (potential) interconnections with all other eternal objects. The traditional doctrine of the absolute isolation of universals is as great a (tacit) error, as the isolation of primary

6. The letter, dated January 2, 1936, appears in *Alfred North Whitehead: Essays on Philosophy*, ed. George L. Kline (Englewood Cliffs, New Jersey: Prentice-Hall, 1963), pp. 196–99 and is reprinted by permission of Prentice-Hall, Inc. I am grateful to Professor Charles Hartshorne and to Whitehead's son, Dr. North Whitehead, for permission to quote from this letter.

substances. The realization of the 'compound individual' involves a finite realization of a complete pattern of eternal objects. The *absolute* abstraction of eternal objects from each other is an analogous error to their abstraction from some mode of realization, and to the abstraction of *res verae* from each other.

v] The simple-minded way in which traditional philosophy —e.g. Hume, Bradley, etc.—has treated universals is the root of all evils. This is the great merit of the *'Gestalt'* people.

William H. Leue has also argued, in his perceptive unpublished study, *Metaphysical Foundations for a Theory of Value in the Philosophy of A. N. Whitehead,*[7] that the charge of Platonism or essentialism neglects the role the principle of coherence plays in Whitehead's metaphysics. And once again I must concede that it is Whitehead's *intent* that the conceptions 'eternal object' and 'actual entity' should furnish a mutual categoreal support.

The rest of this chapter is, then, devoted to an attempt to show that the details of Whitehead's doctrine do not support this intent, and that the category 'eternal object' and the category 'creativity' leave between them little room for the actual entity conceived of as a center of self-creative activity.

The 'realm' of eternal objects: a summary of the relations between eternal objects and between eternal objects and actuality

A short account of Whitehead's explicit views on eternal objects was given in chapter 1. We noticed there that although the eternal objects play in Whitehead's philosophy many of the roles the forms play in Plato's, there are many important differences. The eternal objects are transcendent in the sense that one eternal object may ingress

7. William H. Lene, *Metaphysical Foundation for a Theory of Value in the Philosophy of A. N. Whitehead* (Ph.D. dissertation, 1952, Harvard University Library).

in *many* actual entities, but eternal objects, are, so to speak, made for precisely that role. They are forms of definiteness of actual entities, and thus do not have another and ideal state of being over against which the definiteness of actual entities is somehow deficient. Considered precisely as forms of definiteness, moreover, they form a democracy: for every shade of definiteness of actuality, however mean or perhaps deplorable, there is an eternal object furnishing that definiteness by its ingression. On the explicit level the realm of eternal objects deserves that name 'realm' only because on actual entity—God, considered in his primordial nature—makes them by his 'evisagement' or 'valuation' into an ordered structure that furnishes an ideal for the whole of process.

In that earlier account I mentioned William Christian's list of the examples of eternal objects that Whitehead gives here and there throughout his work, and remarked that the distinction Whitehead makes between the individual essence and the relational essence of eternal objects made for many obscurities. It is said, for instance, that it is by virtue of the individual essence that an eternal object remains precisely the same eternal object through all its ingressions, yet it is by no means clear that when we give an example of an eternal object—as, for example, some particular color—we are focusing only upon an individual essence. In at least one reference to the doctrine of relational essence, Whitehead seems to suggest that any commonplace example of an eternal object is what it is in part by virtue of its relational essence, which is indeed precisely what makes it suitable for ingression in an *extensive* context.

> natural objects require space and time, so that space and time belong to their relational essence without which they cannot be themselves.[8]

8. Alfred North Whitehead, *An Enquiry Concerning the Principles of Natural Knowledge.* 2nd ed. (Cambridge: Cambridge University Press, 1925), p. 202.

It is true that the book in which the passage occurs in a note belongs to Whitehead's pre-metaphysical phase, and that the term 'object' is used in that phase in a wider sense than the later term 'eternal object.' The expression 'natural objects' in the passage just quoted makes this plain. But what are later called eternal objects are *included* in the term 'object,' which indeed at this stage of his philosophy embraces whatever is recognizable and permanent in events.[9] Moreover, the note in question was added to the second (1925) edition of the book, and thus presumably belongs to a time when Whitehead had the doctrine of the relational essences of eternal objects in mind.

In the succeeding sections difficulties of this sort will increase. I may anticipate them by saying that it is by virtue of their relational essences that eternal objects constitute a realm; that their acquiring of relational essences is, according to the intent of Whitehead's account, a function first of God and secondarily of the growth of extensive actual entities; and that apart from their relational essences eternal objects would seem to approach nonentity. And besides these difficulties there is the dominant difficulty that the activity of self-creation by which all actual entities are said to accomplish their concrescence is a questionable one. We are left, I think it will appear, with the conclusion that the acquiring by eternal objects of a gradual enrichment of their relational essences is a process that accounts entirely for the "activity" of the actual entities.

Whitehead tells us that the total multiplicity of Platonic forms, or eternal objects, is not 'given,' and this must seem reasonable enough to us since we have learned that givenness is always the result of the intervention of an actuality. But there are difficulties involved in the further assertion that in respect of each actual entity there is givenness (or relevance of a certain kind) of these forms, for God is also an actual entity.

9. See Christian's chapter 10, "Objects and Events," *op. cit.* pp. 175–92.

Conversely, where there is no decision involving exclusion, there is no givenness. For example, the total multiplicity of Platonic forms is not 'given.' But in respect of each actual entity, there is givenness of such forms. The determinate definiteness of each actuality is an expression of a selection from these forms. It grades them in a diversity of relevance. This ordering of relevance starts from those forms which are, in the fullest sense, exemplified, and passes through grades of relevance down to those forms which in some faint sense are proximately relevant by reason of contrast with actual fact. This whole gamut of relevance is 'given,' and must be referred to the decision of actuality (PR, 69).

The difficulty in question does not hold for extensive actual entities. The passage quoted summarizes in a way our discussion of objectification and real potentiality, and it was perfectly clear how the objectified actuality that is God constitutes a givenness of eternal objects for extensive actual entities, and how these, once objectified, act as powers in turn for future actual entities. For God it is different since, if we abstract from other actual entities, there is nothing to bring about a givenness of eternal objects for him. Must we say that in the case of God we have an exception to Whitehead's rule, and that for him at any rate the total multiplicity of eternal objects *is* given?

Here there is also a question whether when we speak of eternal objects as pure potentials, in abstraction from all actual entities, the word potential is applied with any meaning. It is of course in point here that by potentiality we agree to mean something definite in itself but indeterminate as to the way it will be included in something else. The question can also be put in the form of an objection to the usage "definite in itself" in connection with a potentiality, but such an objection would seem to make most of Whitehead's theory of potentiality meaningless.

Setting this question aside, we are still faced with a considerable difficulty: *a)* if the totality of eternal objects is given to God, then we violate the rule that the totality is never given, and at the same time, by the use of the word 'given' we imply an agency that gives this total-ity; and   *b)* if the *totality* is not given to God, then either there must be *some* givenness of these entities, which also requires agency, or the only status eternal objects have is their subsistence in the primordial nature of God. And yet they seem to be in a sense independent of God in that apart from him they have at least the reality of 'barren, inefficient disjunction.' Such independence would truly require the title potentials (or powers) to be applied to these entities even in such a disjunction; and indeed all other powers would appear as selections among these. It is part of the concern of the present section to determine the meaning of 'barren, inefficient disjunction.'

The question we must now consider therefore is whether eternal objects, in abstraction from all actual entities, are mere non-entities—that is, whether the con-tention that "in separation from actual entities there is nothing, merely nonentity" (PR, 68), applies also to eter-nal objects, which are said to have the kind of existence that allows them to be 'conceptually prehended' or 'men-tally envisaged.' Are we dealing with entities whose exist-ence is to be mentally envisaged, but which if not envis-aged are not real? If so, all potentiality derives ultimately from God, and it is hard to see why we can not refer to him as eminently real. Whitehead's insistence that funda-mental ideas are not abstractable from one another ob-viously, though paradoxically, requires him to give eternal objects a certain independence of all actuality including God, even though he explicitly grants that their whole function is to be prehended in actuality.

But the irreducible polarity of actual entities and eter-nal objects he seeks to maintain has its dangers from the other side. Explicitly he tells us *both* that all reasons must be in terms of actualities (the ontological principle) *and* that actual entities are fluxes of forms or envisagements of forms. There are certain aspects of his thought that tend to make the latter assertion dominate the former, and that within the latter assertion tend to make the image of a *flux* of forms dominate that of an *envisagement* of forms. These aspects are to be found chiefly in the connection between his doctrine of relations and his doctrine of real and general potentiality. To clarify them I shall attempt a deeper study of general and real potentiality than I have so far undertaken.

In chapter x of *Science and the Modern World*[10] he undertakes, under the name 'Abstraction,' a study of the status of eternal objects. In that chapter the term 'abstract entities' is commonly used of the eternal objects, where by 'abstract' he means that "what an eternal object is in itself—that is to say, its essence—is comprehensible without reference to some one particular occasion of experience. To be abstract is to transcend particular concrete occasions of actual happening. But to transcend an actual occasion does not mean being disconnected from it" (smw, 221). The precise sense in which such an entity transcends, but is not disconnected from, actuality is given in the contrast between the individual essence of the eternal object, in virtue of which it transcends any given actuality, and the relational essence, which keeps it from being disconnected from actuality, while permitting it to remain disconnected as to the precise mode of ingression. Whitehead calls these contrasted ideas metaphysical principles, and characterizes them as follows.

> The first principle is that each eternal object is an individual which, in its own peculiar fashion, is what it is. This particular individuality is the individual essence of the object, and cannot be described otherwise than as being itself. Thus the individual essence is merely the essence considered in respect to its uniqueness. Further, the es-

10. In *Science and the Modern World,* as we have seen, what we have come to call real potentiality is taken as belonging to the envisagement of the substantial activity. Although in *Process and Reality* these envisagements belong to God's primordial nature, the view of the relationships within the realm of eternal objects is the same, e.g., the distinction between individual essence and real essence, elaborated in smw, is frequently cited, as is the notion of 'abruptness,' which we shall meet towards the end of the present section.

sence of an eternal object is merely the eternal object considered as adding its own unique contribution to each actual occasion. This unique contribution is identical for all such occasions in respect to the fact that the object in all modes of ingression is just its identical self. But it varies from one occasion to another in respect to the differences of its modes of ingression. Thus the metaphysical status of an eternal object is that of a possibility for an actuality. Every actual occasion is defined as to its character by how these possibilities are actualised for that occasion. Thus actualisation is a selection among possibilities. More accurately, it is a selection issuing in a gradation of possibilites in respect to their realisation in that occasion. This conclusion brings us to the second metaphysical principle: An eternal object, considered as an abstract entity cannot be divorced from its reference to other eternal objects, and from its reference to actuality generally; though it is disconnected from its actual modes of ingression into definite actual occasions. This principle is expressed by the statement that each eternal object has a 'relational essence' (SMW, 222–23).

Our previous doubt whether any genuine meaning can be attached to 'potentiality' in the expression 'general potentiality' apparently does not hold for Whitehead, for an eternal object considered only in its individual essence still is called a possibility, while the distinction between eternal objects considered in their individual essences and the same objects considered also in respect of their relational essences is apparently the difference between general and real potentiality. The meaning of 'barren, inefficient disjunction' in connection with general potentiality is evidently that each eternal object is then considered only in its individual essence, and as such has all its relations, from its side, external. But this is an anticipation, and must await the rest of this section for decision.

There is a correlation made by Whitehead between determinateness and internal relations, and between indeterminateness and external relations. A summary account, in these terms, of the relationships between eternal objects, and between eternal objects and actual entities, may be useful at this point. The context of the account is *real* potentiality rather than *general* potentiality. *a)* Any given eternal object is internally related to every other eternal object, i.e. "In the essence of A [an eternal object] there stands a determinateness as to the relationships of A to other eternal objects . . ." (SMW, 223); this internal relationship of course concerns by definition the relational essence. *b)* Any given eternal object is externally related to actual occasions, these external relations being made possible by the indetermination in its individual essence, which indetermination is nothing more than, as Whitehead says, "its patience for such external relations."

> Again an entity cannot stand in external relations unless in its essence there stands an indeterminateness which is its patience for such external relations. The meaning of the term 'possibility' as applied to A is simply that there stands in the essence of A a patience for relationships to actual occasions (SMW, 223).

It should be noticed that this indetermination concerns only the relations into which the individual essence enters, since it is in itself perfectly determinate and makes an identical "unique contribution" in each ingression by virtue of remaining "just its identical self" (SMW, 222). An eternal object can be thus indeterminate for (or externally related to) an actual entity, and still contribute a definiteness because the "relationships of A [an eternal object] to an actual occasion are simply how the eternal relationships of A to other eternal objects are graded as to their realisation in that occasion" (SMW, 223). That is to say, it is the *internal* [11] relations of an eternal object to other eternal objects, i.e. its relational essence, or 'significance,' [12] that enables it to be an element in the definiteness of an actual occasion, and yet externally related to the actual occasion as regards its individual essence. This is another

11. I think it is possible that in the passage just cited the expression "eternal relationships" is a misprint for "internal relationships," for, as I shall try to show later, there is a sense in which there is a development within the realm of eternal objects—a development, that is, of real potentiality. Quite apart from this consideration, the page in question contains repeated references to the internal relations

way of saying that actuality is a togetherness of forms, or as Whitehead often has it, a 'flux of forms.' And of course it need hardly be said that, from the side of an actual entity, all relations to eternal objects are internal to *it*.

> Thus the synthetic prehension, which is α [an actual occasion], is the solution of the indeterminateness of A [an eternal object] into the determinateness of α. Accordingly the relationship between A and α is external as regards A, and is internal as regards α (smw, 224).

Eternal objects, actuality, and real potentiality

This summary account of the problem of relations has of course been in the field of real potentiality; the summary of the situation—a much simpler one—in general potentiality will be deferred for the moment in favor of a more detailed examination of the implication of actuality in this real potentiality. For the sake of simplicity, the summary did not treat of the way in which the internal relations of an actual occasion to its prehended eternal objects qualifies the relational essences of the latter; an account of real potentiality is incomplete without an examination of this function of actual occasions.

Our account will be nothing more than a repetition of the description of how the objectifications of actual entities (or their satisfactions, their powers) enter into real potentiality. This time, however, the analysis is in terms of relations. I might anticipate its course briefly by saying that relations between eternal objects, between actual occasions (this term always exempts God from its scope), and between eternal objects and actual occasions, are all of them internal, if we consider only the relational essences of eternal objects.[13] If we extend the consideration

between eternal objects. But for the moment the point is unimportant, since the relationships of one eternal object to others, graded as to their realization in an actual occasion, must in any case be internal.
12. smw, 223.
13. What Whitehead means by the 'analytic' character of the realm of eternal objects is dealt with at a later point in the present section.

to all actual entities, and thereby include God in our scope, the situation is the same except that God's primordial nature is externally related, on his side, to other actual entities, his position in this regard being much like the position of the individual essence of an eternal object as over against actual entities. God's valuation of eternal objects *gives* them a relational essence.[14] Actual occasions affect that relational essence further, but the effects of actual occasions upon this real potentiality do not enter internally into God's primordial nature. This is but to say that real potentiality is contained both in God and in the actual world.

The way in which actual occasions enter into relations with the realm of eternal objects, relations which are internal from the side of the eternal objects, is given in the following passage.

> The determinate relatedness of the eternal object A to every other eternal object is how A is systematically and by the necessity of its nature related to every other eternal object. Such relatedness represents a possibility for realisation. But a relationship is a fact which concerns all the implicated relata, and cannot be isolated as if involving only one of the relata. Accordingly there is a general fact of systematic mutual relatedness which is inherent in the character of possibility. . . .
>
> In respect to the ingression of A into an actual occasion α, the mutual relationships of A to other eternal objects, as thus graded in realisation, require for their expression a reference to the status of A and of the other eternal objects in the spatio-temporal relationship. Also this status is not expressible (for this purpose) without a reference to the status of α and of other actual occasions in the same spatio-temporal relationship. Accordingly the spatio-temporal relationship, in terms of which the actual course of events is to be expressed, is nothing else than a selective limitation within the general systematic relationships among eternal objects (SMW, 224–25).

---

14. There is another way of saying this. We may take the term "God" to mean merely that eternal objects, taken as ontological ultimates existing in isolation, have relational essences, and that this gives them existence in a pattern.

This can be taken to mean that the contribution of actual occasions other than God to real potentiality is expressed by the manner in which these actual entities are related to eternal objects with relations that are internal from the side of the eternal objects; or, alternatively, by the manner in which actual occasions qualify the internal relations that eternal objects have among themselves as to their relational essences. It will be recalled that the "relations of *A* [an eternal object] to an actual occasion are simply how the eternal [internal?] relationships of *A* to other eternal objects are graded as to their realisation in that occasion." And similarly, the "general systematic relationships among eternal objects," upon which, in the closing sentences of the last passage quoted, the course of events is said to be a selective limitation, is merely the manner in which eternal objects enter into internal relations (as to their relational essences) with each other in virtue of God's agency. A less friendly interpretation might have it that God (in his primordial nature) is a complex of eternal objects so related.

The contribution (we have questioned whether there is agency involved) to real potentiality by actual entities other than God is, at its most general, the limitations of the extensive continuum upon the "general systematic relationships among eternal objects." Primarily it is "a locus of relational possibility, selected from the more general realm of systematic relationship," which "expresses one limitation of possibility inherent in the general system of the process of realisation" (smw, 225). The problem of the extensive continuum has already been dealt with in another connection.[15] The kind of limitation it sets upon the development of actuality is very pervasive indeed. This does not mean, however, that the course of reality must always be extensive. For one thing the theory of cosmic epochs forbids this conclusion.

In any particular consideration of a possibility we may conceive this continuum to be transcended. But in so far as

15. Chapter 2, section C1.

there is any definite reference to actuality, the definite *how* of transcendence of that spatio-temporal continuum, is required (SMW, 225).

That is to say that a nonextensive state of actuality is not out of the question, but that what that state is to be must take into account the extensiveness of the present cosmic epoch.

Whitehead's theory that real possibility or potentiality involves the internal relatedness of eternal objects introduces the question how finite truth is possible, a question that any doctrine of internal relations must bring in its train. In attempting to cope with this question Whitehead makes several remarks about the status of relational essences that are puzzling, and certainly not on the face of it consistent with my interpretation of the growth of the realm of real potentiality as a growth in the relational essences of a realm of eternal objects. There is no difficulty with the central claim, which is that an eternal object is not merely a sum of internal relations: my interpretation has of course relied heavily on the status of the individual essence. The problem lies rather with the claim that the "relational essence of an object is not unique to that object," the internal relations among eternal objects being "entirely unselective," and "systematically complete" (SMW 229). If this claim meant only that the relational essence (of a given eternal object) does not involve the individual essences of *other* eternal objects, some of the difficulties might disappear. Sometimes Whitehead seems to mean only that, as when in the same passage he says

> Every such relationship of each eternal object is founded upon the perfectly definite status of that object as a relatum in the general scheme of relationships. This definite status is what I have termed the 'relational essence' of that object. This relational essence is determinable by reference to that object alone, and does not require reference to any other objects, except those which are specifically involved in its individual essence when that essence is complex . . . (SMW 229).

Certainly this seems to mean that the relational essence of a given eternal object does depend on its own individual essence as well. If this should be so (and clearly neighboring passages can be interpreted otherwise), it is difficult to see how this does not provide a uniqueness to its relational essence, even though specifying that unique essence should not require us to specify all of the *other* objects it is related to. Whitehead is of course concerned to protect the meaning of the words "any" and "some"—the meaning, as he says, of the variable in logic (SMW, 229). He may thus have diverted himself from his presumed intention to talk in terms of a possibility wider than the merely logical.

Whatever the intent, we are clearly told in this context that "the relational essence of an eternal object is not unique to that object" (SMW, 230). There are difficulties in this for our present interpretation. Some of them we may escape by noting that the chapter in question is a difficult one; that it is earlier than *Process and Reality,* and, though consistent with the latter in many points, perhaps superseded by the general tenor of the discussion in that book of the distinction between general and real potentiality; and that at least part of the discussion in the chapter is oriented more particularly towards real potentiality. Others remain, and the rest of the argument about the status of eternal objects in Whitehead's doctrine must remain tentative in so far as it rests in part upon material from *Science and the Modern World.*

One difficulty lies surely in the ambiguity about the nature of particular eternal objects that we have noticed before. Whitehead's examples are often drawn from sense data: a particular shade of a particular color is frequently mentioned. Yet his frequent observation that eternal objects, apart from the intervention of actuality (including God), constitute a bare and inefficient disjunction that approaches nonentity, make us wonder whether *any* particular example of an eternal object that we might offer must not include a relational as well as individual essence. He frequently remarks that the characteristics of the extensive continuum constitute the widest framework of real potentiality.[16] The extensive continuum is therefore the result of actuality (including God). It therefore in some sort goes back to the relationships that exist between eternal objects in God's primordial nature; and if a particular shade of color is meaningless apart from some reference to this continuum, there must be *something* of relatedness in the very uniqueness of that particular shade.

Whitehead evidently wishes to guard the status we usually accord any universal, namely, that it should be the *same* universal in all its appearances: hence his identification of that which is unique in the eternal object with its individual essence. The foregoing argument casts some doubt upon this, and it is lent some support by the note quoted earlier from Whitehead's *Principles of Natural Knowledge*, in which the possibility of an object's ingression in an extensive situation is associated with the relational essence. Another passage from the very late letter to Charles Hartshorne that was quoted awhile ago shows him concerned even towards the end *both* with the individual essence as the bearer of the uniqueness of the eternal object *and* with the theme of the *growth* of the relational essence with the march of actuality.

> no eternal object in any finite realization can exhibit the full potentialities of its nature. It has an individual essence—whereby it is the same eternal object on diverse occasions, and it has a relational essence whereby it has an infinitude of modes of entry into realization. But realization introduces finitude (in Spinoza's sense), with the extension of the infinitude of incompatibles in the relational essence.[17]

If there remains much that is obscure in this matter, it is at any rate clear that Whitehead has given in many similar passages a sense in which the march of actuality qualifies real potentiality. It would appear to be plausible that the

16. E.g. smw, 226.
17. George L. Kline, *op. cit.*, p. 199.

consequent growth of relational essences is what *makes* an eternal object the *kind* of eternal object that can ingress in a certain context.

But I do not think that these considerations can be used to counter the charge of Platonism that I have made. For even if eternal objects without their relational essences verge on nonentity, and even if any particular eternal object we can identify is identifiable in part by virtue of its relational essence, it is still true *a)* that relational essences are dependent upon individual essences, which are thus (as we shall see in the sequel) ontological ultimates; and *b)* that the march of actuality—the very concrescence of actual entities, the very growth of real potentiality—can be accounted for in terms of the growth of relational essences.

We may now return to the question of finite truth. There are two passages in which Whitehead's solution of the problem of finite truth is summarized.

> The *analytical character* of the realm of eternal objects is the primary metaphysical truth concerning it. By this character it is meant that the status of any eternal object *A* in this realm is capable of analysis into an indefinite number of subordinate relationships of limited scope (smw, 228).

> The difficulty inherent in the concept of finite internal relations among eternal objects is thus evaded by two metaphysical principles, *i*] that the relationships of any eternal object *A*, considered as constitutive of *A*, merely involve other eternal objects as bare relata without reference to their individual essences, and *ii*] that the divisibility of the general relationship of *A* into a multiplicity of finite relationships of *A* stands therefore in the essence of that eternal object. The second principle obviously depends upon the first. To understand *A* is to understand the *how* of a general scheme of relationship. This scheme of relationship does not require the individual uniqueness of the other relata for its comprehension. This scheme also discloses itself as being analysable into a multiplicity of limited relationships which have their own individuality

and yet at the same time presupposes the total relationship within possibility (SMW, 231).

He goes on to point out that not all eternal objects are simple. Any finite segment of real potentiality, "involving the definite eternal objects of a limited set of such objects" (SMW, 232), constitutes a complex eternal object. As such the distinction between relational and individual essence again holds: the complex eternal object A will have its relational essence expressing its involvement in a wider complex eternal object, B, into which wider relational essence the relational essences of the components of A will presumably enter; and the complex eternal object A will have a complex individual essence. But this last means only, as regards the component eternal objects, that "in respect to some of their possible relationships there is a togetherness of their individual essences" (SMW, 230). Here Whitehead is talking of the real togetherness in a given actual occasion, but it can be made to fit the present occasion if we add that the togetherness is not *real* but *possible;* in which case it is merely another way of saying that the eternal objects forming parts of a complex eternal object enter into internal relations with each other only in respect of their relational essences.

The account of real potentiality has been first given in terms of the theory of objectifications, and then elaborated and made more precise by reiteration in terms of the internal relations acquired by eternal objects. The account has fitly included some remarks in terms of complex eternal objects, because the theory of real potentiality is given perhaps its most fine-spun elaboration in terms of what Whitehead calls 'abstractive hierarchies,' and these abstractive hierarchies are a kind of complex eternal object. After a summary of the doctrine of abstractive hierarchies, the present section can be completed by drawing the conclusions about the ultimate status of eternal objects towards which we have been moving.

The doctrine of abstractive hierarchies is designed to "explain how the analytical character of the realm of eternal objects allows of an analysis of that realm into grades" (smw, 232). Or we can say that it is the story how real potentiality can be considered as a 'graduation of relevance.' An abstractive hierarchy is defined as the route of progress in thought through successive grades of increasing complexity toward "some assigned mode of abstraction from the realm of possibility" (smw, 234). Here abstraction is toward a high degree of complexity in the eternal object in question. Such abstraction from possibility is not abstraction from actuality, and is therefore more complex as it approaches more closely the full concreteness of an actual occasion, if we happen to be dealing with an abstractive hierarchy so founded upon an actual occasion as to be called an 'associated hierarchy.'

> In any actual occasion α, there will be a group g of simple eternal objects which are ingredient in that group in the most concrete mode. This complete ingredience in an occasion, so as to yield the most complete fusion of individual essence with other eternal objects in the formation of the individual emergent occasion, is evidently of its own kind and cannot be defined in terms of anything else. But is has a peculiar characteristic which necessarily attaches to it. This characteristic is that there is an *infinite* abstractive hierarchy based upon g which is such that all its members are equally involved in this complete inclusion in. . . . I will call this infinite abstractive hierarchy which is associated with α 'the associated hierarchy of α' (smw, 237).

Whitehead likens this to an 'elaborate logical construction'[18] (smw, 238), and it can be thought of as the (inexhaustible) description of the definiteness of an actual occasion, or, because it is such, the (inexhaustible) account of how the togetherness of eternal objects which is that particular actual occasion sets its stamp upon the real potentiality with which some future entity is to be

18. The parallel with Bertrand Russell's language is striking. The relations between the doctrines of the two men in fields other than formal logic can, I suggest, be examined with some profit. But the job requires someone better versed in Russell's work than I am.

confronted.[19] The description of the definiteness of an actual entity involves all eternal objects, in a gradation of relevance, so that its conditioning of real potentiality is also described in terms of a gradation. To describe it fully we have to tell how all entities in the universe are prehended by it, positively or negatively, with important or faint relevance. And we must also tell how the entities in question are interrelated by the fact that they are all prehended by just this actual occasion; this interrelation constitutes a conditioning of potentiality.

That an abstractive hierarchy so characterized is an infinite one means that, however great a degree of complexity of these interrelations we may specify, analysis will always reveal further complexities. The requirement of infinitude here has to do with the degree of complexity of what we may call a description either of the actual occasion or of the stamp that actual occasion sets upon real potentiality. It does not mean that the occasion is not perfectly definite or that the potentiality is not definitely qualified by it.

The requirement of infinitude here may be clearer when contrasted with the next topic: the notion of a finite complex eternal object. This notion expresses how real potentiality enters into an actual entity in a way such that that entity neither has in respect of it the full definiteness it would have as a satisfied actual entity, nor qualifies it in the full degree we have noticed in dealing with associated abstractive hierarchies. The theory of abstractive hierarchies that are finite complex eternal objects sets forth the way in which the mental pole of an actual entity in process exhibits a certain kind of ingression of eternal objects. The theory therefore describes how the mental pole qualifies real potentiality.

19. The following quotation is pertinent. "We conceive actuality as in essential relation to an unfathomable possibility. Eternal objects inform actual occasions with hierarchic patterns, included and excluded in every variety of discrimination. Another view of the same truth is that every actual occasion is a limitation imposed on possibility, and that by virtue of this limitation the particular value of that shaped togetherness of things emerges" (SMW, 243–44). "It

Now the mental pole is the pole of the entity in which its future resides. It is therefore asserted to be, as we have seen, the factor of freedom or novelty in Whitehead's metaphysics, although in chapters 3 and 4 its right to the title was criticized. If the mental pole qualifies real potentiality, it is exerting a certain kind of power, and therefore contains its future and contains it as a power. The reader will recall, from chapters 1 and 2, that such a notion was necessary if an entity is to be called in any sense free. But here we shall once more have in mind the absence of active power, and will give attention to the fact that the qualification of real potentiality by the mental pole is the exertion of power in a sense analogous to the existence *objectivé* of a settled actual entity. That is, the qualification of real potentiality will be seen to be by way of a configuration or togetherness of eternal objects, the configuration being of a sort different from that of full actuality. Once more, the configuration of eternal objects making up the mental pole will be held to emerge either *a)* as a product of prior configurations, including that of the primordial nature of God, or *b)* in part arbitrarily, from nowhere, as a new configuration of eternal objects, whose whole existence *is* that configuration. But however questionable the conditioning of real potentiality by the mental pole of an actual entity may be as a freedom factor, it is necessary to finish the account of it in order to complete our account of Whitehead's view of the status of actuality as over against eternal objects.

The full concreteness of an actual entity is, then, contrasted with the mental pole by the fact that in the case of the former the ingression of eternal objects involves an associated abstractive hierarchy that is infinite; while in the case of the latter there is a prehension of one or more finite abstractive hierarchies. Thus an actual occasion,

is in respect to its associated hierarchy, as displayed in this immediate present, that an occasion finds its own originality. It is that display which is its own contribution to the output of actuality" (smw, 246). We have of course been asking just *what* contributes in this way, and have been suggesting that the actuality is merely the emergence of togetherness, rather than the shaping of it.

being "a prehension of one infinite hierarchy (its associated hierarchy) together with various finite hierarchies"
(smw, 239–40), must condition real potentiality one way
in respect of the first, and another in respect of the second.
The following passage is in terms proper to mental experience, but of course Whitehead's sense is the wider one of
'mental pole,' in which no consciousness is necessarily
present.

> A complete occasion includes that which in cognitive ex-
> perience takes the form of memory, anticipation, imagina-
> tion, and thought. These elements in an experient occa-
> sion are also modes of inclusion of complex eternal objects
> in the synthetic prehension, as elements in the emergent
> value. They differ from the concreteness of full inclusion.
> In a sense this difference is inexplicable; for each mode of
> inclusion is of its own kind, not to be explained in terms of
> anything else. But there is a common difference which
> discriminates these modes of inclusion from the full con-
> crete ingression which has been discussed. This *differentia*
> is *abruptness*. By 'abruptness' I mean that what is remem-
> bered, or anticipated, or imagined, or thought, is ex-
> hausted by a finite complex concept. In each case there is
> one finite eternal object prehended within the occasion as
> the vertex of a finite hierarchy. This breaking off from an
> actual illimitability is what in any occasion marks off that
> which is termed mental from that which belongs to the
> physical event to which the mental functioning is referred
> (smw, 238–39).

Elsewhere,[20] this abruptness is equated with the notion
of graded envisagement, which we have already encountered. There is a difficult problem here, for this graded
envisagement has a double function with respect to real
potentiality. The finite abstractive hierarchy prehended
constitutes both a qualification of the actual occasion,

20. "This abrupt synthesis of eternal objects in each occasion is the
inclusion in actuality of the analytical character of the realm of
eternality. This inclusion has those limited gradations of actuality
which characterise every occasion by reason of its essential limitation. It is this realised extension of eternal relatedness beyond the
mutual relatedness of the actual occasions, which prehends into each
occasion the full sweep of eternal relatedness. I term this abrupt

without entering into its full concreteness, and a qualification of the real potentiality, without entering into *that* as
the objectification or satisfaction of a real concrescence. If
we take as an example an appetition in a given actual
entity, we should have to say that it both qualifies the
realm of potentiality that is available to all other actual
entities and to itself and is the means by which real
potentiality becomes the settled fact of that particular
actual entity. The meaning becomes much clearer if one
thinks of the types of feelings that can make up the
mental pole of an actual entity: propositional feelings,
contrasts, physical purposes, may all of them serve as
illustrations. The following quotation is in terms of the
last.

> The mental operations have a double office. They achieve,
> in the immediate subject, the subjective aim of that sub-
> ject as to the satisfaction to be obtained from its own
> initial data. In this way the decision derived from the
> actual world, which is the efficient cause, is completed by
> the decision embodied in the subjective aim which is the
> final cause. Secondly, the physical purposes of a subject by
> their valuations determine the relative efficiency of the
> various feelings to enter into the objectifications of that
> subject in the creative advance beyond itself. In this
> function, the mental operations determine their subject in
> its character of an efficient cause. Thus the mental pole is
> the link whereby the creativity is endowed with the dou-
> ble character of final causation and efficient causation. The
> mental pole is constituted by the decisions in virtue of
> which matters of fact enter into the character of the
> creativity (PR, 423).

Here "enter into the character of the creativity" means
"condition real potentiality"—for this is all the character
creativity has.

realisation the 'graded envisagement' which each occasion prehends
into its synthesis. This graded envisagement is how the actual
includes what (in one sense) is not-being as a positive factor in its
own achievement. It is the source of error, of truth, of art, of ethics,
and of religion. By it, fact is confronted with alternatives" (SMW,
247).

The above discussion of the mental pole is directed to the wider question of the effects upon potentiality of the march of actuality. Some further remarks on subjective aim, though indeed relevant to this question, will also widen the vista somewhat and incidentally help complete our earlier discussion of subjective aim.

One way of characterizing subjective aim is to say that it is the subjective form with which a proposition is felt.[21] A subjective form can, however, be understood in terms of the subjective species of eternal objects.[22] This then permits us to think of the qualification of real potentiality by the mental pole in the following terms. *a)* It is a complex eternal object that includes some components that belong to the subjective species. *b)* The complex is a finite abstractive hierarchy and the determinateness of the internal relations among the components falls therefore somewhat short of what we should have in full actuality. *c)* In so far as the mental pole is efficacious in the transition from the indeterminate to the settled, the components of the finite abstractive hierarchy are already internally related in a way that qualifies them as to the later relations they will enter into in the infinite abstractive hierarchy that is associated with the entity at the completion of its passage. *d)* The relations among the components of the resultant infinite hierarchy more fully qualify real potentiality than do those of any finite hierarchy.

Transition here wears a very static aspect, and it is at least possible to think of it in terms of a shuffling of eternal objects in which these acquire internal relations that permanently qualify their aptitude for further relations, and in which the very character of the successiveness that makes us think of this togetherness of eternal objects as a flux is regulated in part by internal relations already entered into.

We have been approaching the problem of freedom in such a way as to imply that it may well be reducible to the fact that *some* of the internal relations that eventually come about are not so regulated, but come about arbitrar-

21. PR, 37.
22. See chapter 2, section D.

ily and without ground. On this view creativity embodies only the metaphysical principle that there is a flux that issues in togetherness of a very determinate kind. This suggestion depends upon the analysis of creativity in chapter 4, and expresses only the consequence of taking that analysis together with the present analysis of the realm of eternal objects.

It might be objected that for Whitehead real togetherness is always togetherness in a feeling. On this objection, the assertion that subjective form is nothing more than an eternal object of the subjective species would not be quite accurate, unless we were to add that, in so characterizing it, we are abstracting it from a feeling. But after all, what does it mean to be in a feeling? Let us take up again the earlier discussion of contrasts.[23]

A contrast is the kind of unity components have in a feeling, and I suggest that this kind of unity can be described entirely—if this interpretation of creativity is valid—in terms of eternal objects that are together in a certain way. It will be remembered that unity of components in a prehension was a unity in which there was a real diversity of status of the components combined with a genuine synthesis. Such a unity was held to be no mere togetherness, no "mere collective disjunctive of component elements" (PR, 349), and in designating it as a contrast provision was made both for the real discreteness of the terms, and for their real internal relations. I submit that no other definition of 'togetherness in a feeling' is offered by Whitehead; and that, in the absence of a doctrine of active power that would give us a subject *for* the feelings, we must construe feelings that aim at their subject as "components together in a contrast." It is just at this point that it becomes quite clear why the notion of superject is preferred: a superject is a contrast of components, where the components are reducible ultimately to eternal objects.[24]

23. See chapter 2, section Cɪɪɪ.
24. Besides the discussion of 'contrasts' just cited, these conclusions presuppose the role of eternal objects of the objective species. See chapter 2, sections Aɪ, Aɪɪ, D.

General potentiality: eternal objects as ontological ultimates

So much being said, we may now turn to the question of general potentiality. Here the subject of individual essence will again come to the fore, and its analysis will permit a final return to the topic of general potentiality to reveal precisely what is meant by 'power' when we say that an entity's contribution to real potentiality, or its objectification, constitutes its power. The purpose is to exhibit all such power as derivative from eternal objects, and therefore to suggest that, although Whitehead explicitly claims that abstract and concrete entities have coeval status, the details of his theory reveal a prejudice in favor of the ultimacy of abstract entities.

Any imaginable relation among eternal objects, for instance "opposite of" or "contrary of," is an internal relation, having to do with relational rather than individual essence. If we divorce eternal objects from the course of actuality, including God, we strip them of even such basic relations as these, and it becomes hard to say just what status the eternal objects would then have. It is clear that actuality does not in any way affect the individual essence, and indeed it appears that the individual essence's capacity for external relations signifies a kind of independence of ontological status denied all other entities whatsoever.

Whitehead expresses this independence in many ways, but principally in the conceptions of the 'Isolation of Eternal Objects' and 'The Translucency of Realisation.' These are not exactly equivalent notions, but rather stress two different aspects of the independence of individual essences (or their patience for external relations). Eternal objects are said to be isolated in the realm of possibility "because their relationships as possibilities are expressible without reference to their respective individual essences" (SMW, 230). Their realization is said to be translucent because "any eternal object is just itself in whatever mode of realisation it is involved. There can be no distortion of the individual essence without thereby producing a different eternal object. In the essence of each eternal object there stands an indeterminateness which expresses its indifferent patience for any mode of ingression into any actual occasion" (SMW, 240). The independence of each of the eternal objects appears to remain even though we choose to call general potentiality a 'barren, inefficient disjunction' (PR, 64) or 'boundless, abstract possibility' (PR, 336), for 'disjunction' from other objects and 'possibility' together give precisely the meaning of 'individual essence.'

Our most telling point here is that neither God nor any other actual entity creates the individual essence of an eternal object.

> He does not create eternal objects; for his nature requires them in the same degree that they require him. This is an exemplification of the coherence of the categoreal types of existence. The general relationships of eternal objects to each other, relationships of diversity and of pattern, are their relationships in God's conceptual realisation. Apart from this realisation, there is mere isolation indistinguishable from nonentity (PR, 392).

There are various difficulties in the quotation. What, for instance, does it mean to say that God does not create eternal objects, or that there are no new eternal objects, and then to add that without God there is "mere isolation indistinguishable from nonentity"? Again, if eternal objects, in their individual essences, enter into relations that are always external and never internal from their side, is it not also possible to say that God, although related externally to other actual entities, is related internally to eternal objects? His relation to them is determinate and static; it is frequently described as a satisfaction, or an objectification; and it is often said to be a valuation, or kind of feeling. One must remember that God, no less than any actual occasion, can be described, as in the conclusion to the previous section, as a certain kind of togetherness of eternal objects. It is true that while Whitehead speaks of components being together in the feeling of an actual occasion, he speaks of togetherness in God's 'envisagement' or 'valuation.' But the same strictures that were applied to the notion of feeling are applicable to these notions, which indeed appear to be variants of 'feeling.' To say, as I do here, that God's primordial nature is internally related to eternal objects, is only to say that it is possible to reduce the conception of God to that of a pattern of eternal objects.

I should like to suggest that for a philosophy like Whitehead's an entity that has power (in his meaning) is one with a patience for external relations; and that if such an entity has a patience for external relations only, it consists of nothing but power. Such a description applies only to eternal objects (taken in their individual essences), and on its showing entities other than the eternal objects have power by entering into relations with eternal objects, these relations being external from the side of the eternal objects, internal from the side of the entity in question. Possession of power for entities other than eternal objects consists in a patience for external relations resulting from the fact that these entities include a determinate togetherness of eternal objects in an aesthetic synthesis.

But as this aesthetic synthesis is in turn reducible to a pattern of eternal objects, we can really carry the point further. As we observed in the previous section, an actual entity is not merely internally related to eternal objects, it can in fact be thought of as *consisting of* a pattern of eternal objects in which the latter take on a permanent qualification of their relational essences. These relational essences are made up, in turn, of internal relations, so that it appears that the capacity for entering into external relations (and thus the capacity for exercising power) goes back ultimately to the individual essences of eternal objects. We have already noticed how oddly this side of Whitehead's doctrine goes with the claim that eternal objects without their relational essences verge on nonentity.

This description of power applies to any objectification, whether of God or of actual occasions, since the
possibility of objectification—that which constitutes an
entity as an object—is its patience for relations, external
from its side, with other actual occasions. The notion of an
object as a datum for feeling is important here: eternal
objects taken as individual essences are data for feeling,
and *only* that, because they can be related only externally;
God is a datum for feeling because he is externally related
to other actual entities (in this guise he supplies initial
subjective aim); and any given actual entity other than
God is a datum for feeling because it can enter into
external relations with subsequent actual entities. In each
case, the felt actual entity's character as a datum for
feeling is traceable to the character of eternal objects and
thus ultimately to their individual essences. In each case
the entity that feels an objectified entity acquires internal
relations to the latter. And status as object, which enables
an objectified entity to stand in external relations to the
actual entity that feels it, depends upon the internal relations the objectified entity has to eternal objects.

Object status, or status as a power, can be called
derivative, passive, perceptive, or superjective. The terms
have somewhat the same meaning, but vary in the extent
to which they suggest that substantival entities are involved. Thus to say that an actual entity is a power
because it is perceptive of other powers, is to suggest—
what we have denied—that the entities in question are
other than togethernesses of eternal objects. If we call
Whitehead's doctrine of freedom a radical finalism, we
suggest that any real togetherness of eternal objects is
derivative from prior ones—including God's primordial
nature as prior. If we offer an alternative interpretation in
terms of radical origination, we suggest that—failing the
presence of a subject as an active power—there is radical
origination of real togetherness of eternal objects. But in
either case the superjective side is to the fore: there can
only be combinations, whether new in the extensive
world, or radically new, of entities themselves eternal. On
the alternative described as "radical origination" the ap-

pearance of such combinations is arbitrary. Our main point against the doctrine of freedom, then, appears to be that the actual entities alleged to possess freedom lack a genuine entitative character: the sense in which they exist is derivative from the sense in which essences, or abstract entities, or eternal objects, exist. And not the least reason for this charge is that the actual entities are capable only derivatively of standing in external relations.

The role of God's primordial nature

We shall now apply the conclusions of the preceding section more closely to God's primordial nature in an attempt to show the effect his status has upon the status of extensive actual entities.

An actual entity is said to be free in virtue of its mental pole, or subjective aim. God in his primordial nature consists wholly of a mental pole, but one can hardly say more of his freedom than that it is a certain kind of free togetherness of eternal objects, the togetherness being described as an envisagement, or valuation. Now such a togetherness is certainly free in the sense that no other grounds can be given for it; and Whitehead is certainly entitled to choose it as an ultimate and designate it as the standard of freedom. But we are entitled to ask whether the question "What is free?" can be adequately answered in terms of the conception that the feeling is what it is so that the feeler may be what he is (PR, 339). I suggest that the logic of this conception leads us eventually to hold that the component eternal objects are what they are, and are together as they are, so that the feeling may be what it is. "God as the standard of freedom" seems to be identical with "arbitrary complex of eternal objects, together in a 'contrast.' "

Knowing as we do that the mental pole of extensive actual entities, or actual occasions, is at least partially dependent upon this aspect of God, we can call their freedom in question. We can think of God's primordial nature as a real togetherness of eternal objects that produces the real togetherness that we call extensive actual entities, except where such real togetherness might be thought to come to pass arbitrarily, in partial independence of God, and in spite of his persuasion. But we must observe how the character of the primordial nature infects the 'entities' that it wholly or partially produces. It is important that there is no action in God's primordial nature: even in his character of principle of concretion he does not put forth energy. The new entity is rather a growing together of a new set of feelings, one of which, as we have seen, is a hybrid feeling of God, by way of God's feeling for the *impasse* out of which the new entity grows, and this *being felt* as an element in a new togetherness of feelings, is the sole function of God. We have perhaps sufficiently questioned the appropriateness of using the word "feeling" in this way. The static character of God is carried over to the mental pole of the new concrescence, and we have seen this situation reflected in the description of the mental pole as a group of finite abstractive hierarchies. Such a description explains some of the problems encountered in chapter 3 in connection with the modification of subjective aim. There we took the theory in its professed character of a dynamism and encountered difficulties that culminated in our examination of creativity; here the static character of subjective aim appears with clarity enough, and makes us aware of the incongruousness of trying to get a dynamism out of so extreme an essentialism.

It is peculiar to a philosophy of this sort that, on the one hand, the nearest approach to an ultimate ground why things are as they are must be expressed as an envisagement of eternal objects that is independent of the eternal objects in the sense that they do not produce it; while, on the other hand, this ultimate must be understandable in terms of an interconnectedness of eternal objects, there being no other kind of entity that is a power. God's whole status as a valuation can presumably be given in terms of eternal objects of the subjective species, for God no less than other actual entities has a subjective aim, and his prehensions of eternal objects and of actual entities (his consequent nature) has a subjective form.[25] He is a 'conceptual harmonization'[26] whose inner harmony we cannot express otherwise than in a concept. Consider the following description of God's primordial nature.

> The 'primordial nature' of God is the concrescence of a unity of conceptual feelings, including among their data all eternal objects. The concrescence is directed by the subjective aim, that the subjective forms of the feelings shall be such as to constitute the eternal objects into relevant lures of feelings severally appropriate for all realizable basic conditions (PR, 134).

We have of course seen long since that subjective form is given in terms of eternal objects of the subjective species. But the point will be clearer if it is noticed that the 'unity of conceptual feelings' mentioned above is a unity of subjective aim, and if the following description of subjective aim is taken into account.

> the concrescence of a *res vera* is the development of a subjective aim. This development is nothing else than the Hegelian development of an idea (PR, 254).[27]

The whole character of actuality, including the process that belongs to extensive actualities, here appears as a togetherness of eternal objects. For God the matter is crucial: that which in him is beyond eternal objects and which is sometimes (perhaps unguardedly) spoken of almost as though it conferred existence on eternal objects, is given in terms of the togetherness of eternal objects. For extensive actual entities, in which we find no active substantival power, and which issue from a creativity characterized only by the static power furnished by infinite and finite abstractive hierarchies, i.e. by real poten-

25. PR, 161, 523, 525.
26. PR, 526.
27. Whitehead is here talking of an extensive actual entity; moreover he would repudiate an ultimate Hegelian prejudice. But the inadvertence is perhaps significant, and perhaps more so for the case of God than for that of actual occasions.

tiality and determinate subjective aims, the case is the same: process appears to be not only presided over, but also identical with, a complex togetherness of abstract entities. Either there is a radical finalism founded on God, or there is the appearance *ex nihilo* of an arbitrary real togetherness of abstract entities. In either case the super-jective side of actual entities (including God) quite re-places the subject side.

Recapitulation of the argument of chapters 5 and 6

The chief theme of these chapters was that the empha-sis Whitehead lays upon actual entities, an emphasis ex-pressed in his ontological principle ("no actual entity, then no reason"), is considerably diminished by the privi-leged status he gives eternal objects. He appears, in fact, to ascribe to the latter more of the traditional marks of substantiality than he does to actual entities. The develop-ment of this theme presupposed the earlier discussions of creativity, in which it was argued that creativity was not the source of an active power, and that the idea of an actual entity as a *self*-creative *subject* was therefore an untenable one. The present argument completes the ear-lier one by showing that the only powers in Whitehead's system are those of eternal objects.

Much of our argument was devoted to the status of eternal objects as potentials for definiteness, and to the equivalence of this notion to 'power, indeterminate as to its exercise.' On the ontological principle, one would ex-pect that real potentiality came about by the action of the power of actual entities upon general potentiality. It was contended, however, that the so-called power of actual entities was simply the power of eternal objects when these are together in a certain kind of relatedness. This contention was supported by an analysis of the relations between eternal objects taken as defining real potentiality, and of the relations between these eternal objects and actual entities. As a result of this analysis it was maintained that the story of the functioning of actual entities was reducible to the story of the gradual development of real potentiality as it becomes further qualified by infinite and finite abstractive hierarchies. And if this development is not merely an apparent one (not, that is, a radical finalism determined by the initial qualification of potentiality by God's primordial nature), it is ascribable to the final self-creative reaction of the universe only in the sense that it comes to pass or happens "without reason" and not in the sense that it is a function of the *self*-creation of actual entities. Analysis of the development of internal relations within the realm of eternal objects was not therefore merely an *alternative* view of the agency of actual entities, but in fact left no room for any useful conception of such agency.

The real togetherness in a feeling that is, according to Whitehead, productive of the kind of togetherness of eternal objects that permanently qualifies real potentiality appeared on the present interpretation nothing more than the togetherness of eternal objects in a contrast, failing an active power in self-creation that might shape these feelings. Togetherness of eternal objects in a contrast was, to be sure, no *mere* togetherness in that entities otherwise discrete are really synthesized, but the significance of real synthesis appeared to be exhausted by the internal relations (with respect to relational essences) acquired by eternal objects in the course of creativity. The ultimate importance of the term 'superject' as over against 'subject' was therefore insisted upon throughout the argument. It was held that a superjective actual entity was merely a contrast of components, where the components are reducible ultimately to eternal objects, and where all power said to be exercised by an actual entity is a superjective power ascribable ultimately to eternal objects. This point assumes that the term 'creativity' merely embodies the metaphysical principle that there is a flux that issues in a determinate togetherness of eternal objects.

The contention that eternal objects are the ontological ultimate of Whitehead's system, and in particular that all

senses of 'power' are derivative from them, culminated in
an examination of the relation between God's primordial
nature and eternal objects. It was held that God's primordial nature could be adequately described as a structure
of eternal objects that are internally related as regards
their relational essences. The distinction between the individual essence and the relational essence was important
here as throughout the chapters; in particular, the status
of eternal objects as ontological ultimates was held to
depend on these characteristics of the individual essences:
they are uncreated; they can enter into external relations;
and there are no new ones.

Index

INDEX

Accident, 130, 131, 137, 157

Activity, substantial, 127–30, 139, 168n

Actual entity: as concrescence, vi, 98, 107, 109; finite, vii; as self-creation, vii, 93, 131, 163; definition of, 3, 4, 6; and subjectivity, 10–17; and subjective aim, 12–17, 91, 104; and creativity, 12–17, 102; mental pole of, 25–42; physical pole of, 25–42; definiteness of, 37, 38, 52, 164; and determination, 38, 102, 149; genetic division of, 44–47, 81, 83; coordinate division of, 44–47, 81, 141; satisfaction of, 44, 49, 57, 67n, 69, 75, 81, 91, 91n, 96, 97, 111, 112, 120, 122, 171, 183; and conformation, 55–57, 71; and indetermination, 87, 93; and eternal objects, 87, 149, 160, 162, 187, 191, 193; extensive, 97, 118, 155, 190; activity (agency) of, 104, 153, 161, 162; and *haecceitas*, 118; and objectification, 135, 145, 149, 171; and internal relations, 140; existence *objectivé* of, 181; and external relations, 190. *See also* Feeling; Self-Creation; Subject; Subject-superject; Superject

Actuality: cell-theory of, 31; and subject-superject, 74; and potentiality, 123, 145, 150, 185; and extensiveness, 127, 174, 176; Aristotle and Whitehead compared on, 145; and form, 162; and external objects, 163–79, 192; mentioned, 130, 131, 132

Actual occasion, vi, 3, 4, 5, 6, 18, 73, 128, 129, 135, 173. *See also,* Actual entity

Actual world: and objectification, 42, 43–44, 74; and potentiality, 84–98, 89; mentioned, 6, 12, 33n, 34, 41, 87, 130, 151, 152, 183

Adventures of Ideas (Whitehead), v, 81–82n, 58

Agency: of comparison, 147, 152, 156; of actual entity, 151, 153, 157; and givenness, 167; God's, 173; reality of questioned, 194

Alexander, Samuel, 104

Alfred North Whitehead: Essays on His Philosophy (Kline, ed.), viii, 77n, 54, 162n

Aristotle: on *ousiai*, 7; on matter, 127, 134, 136; on potentiality, 146; and Whitehead, 159, 160; on actuality 161

Becoming: act of, 47, 48, 104; and epochal theory of time, 46–48; continuity of, 48. *See also,* Epochal theory of time

Bergson, Henri, 10–14, 15, 19, 20, 132, 133, 134

Bradley, F. H., 53, 163

Categoreal Obligation: of Freedom and Determination, 14, 17; of Conceptual Valuation, 37, 58–60, 88; of Conceptual Reversion, 38, 58–60; of Transmutation, 58, 59; of Subjective Intensity, 60; of Subjective Harmony, 103; of Subjective Unity, 103; mentioned, 37, 103

Category: of the Ultimate, 18, 26, 30, 133, 161; of Existence, 34; of Explanation, 34, 38, 61,